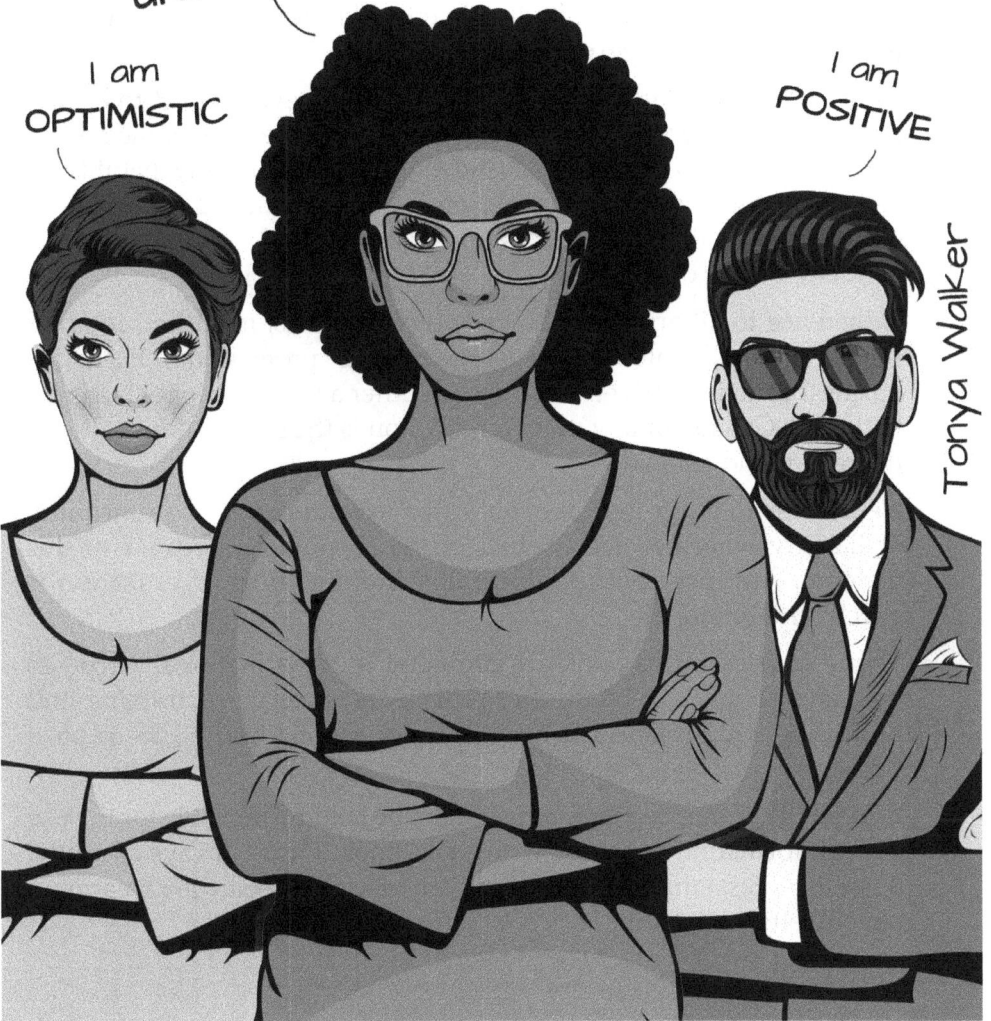

TABLE OF CONTENTS

DEDICATION

This book is dedicated to God for birthing *You Don't Define Me*. To my husband, Damon Walker Sr., who encouraged and pushed me to write the book. To my son, Demond Walker, who helped me by reading chapters and giving input when needed. To my son, Damon Walker Jr., for believing in me.

We are a Family of Strength, Created by Faith, United in Love, and Preserved by I Am.

— Tonya Walker

INTRODUCTION

Change your conception of yourself and you will automatically change the world in which you live. Do not try to change people; they are only messengers telling you who you are. Revalue yourself and they will confirm the change.

— Neville Goddard

How would you like to finally conquer your fears, be happy for the majority of your life rather than being sad for the majority of your life, live in faith vs fear, and accomplish your goals? What if I was able to prove that you do not have to depend on anyone, live in shame, or be a slave to anyone or anything to have the life that you want?

I know what you are thinking: just another book about does and don'ts, right and wrong, or someone just judging you. No, this book is designed to help you accomplish your fears in real time, be happy the majority of the time you have on Earth, teaches you how to live in faith vs fear to push you towards the life you want, and helps you accomplish your goals.

Guess what? I have the proven skills, knowledge, and practices you need to make it happen. Would you be willing to listen, put in the work, and follow through to the end? Just to be completely honest, if you do not make this way of living a lifestyle, it will be so easy to return to the life that you do not want. To be truthful, you must make this lifestyle a habit just like anything else in life. No one is perfect and can start going back down the wrong road at any time.

This book will teach you how to get back on the right path quickly, so it does not mess up your God-given destiny.

Through the course of this book, you will learn how to stand on your own two feet, how to love yourself completely, to overcome the daily distractions that keep you going down the wrong road, and how to define yourself.

How is it that a person's life can change in a moment? How is it that a person can be doing fine one minute, suddenly falls into a trap the next and not know how they got there? How is it that a person ends up living the life they never wanted to live and do things they never imagined doing? I can answer these questions. They have allowed people, church members, coworkers, managers, parents, teachers, certain relationships, bad experiences, situations, circumstances, and their own mind define who they are in life.

You Don't Define Me helps you discover the power within you – the power that allows you to accomplish everything you desire in life. We all have this power, but sometimes we fail to see it because we are looking at ourselves through other peoples' eyes. Inner power is available to us all, but the only ones that use this power are the ones that are aware of the power.

Nothing comes from without; all things come from within.

— Neville Goddard.

You can move past the things that are currently defining you and find a better way. I know this because I have been through it. God brought me through several tough experiences, but each one taught me more about defining myself. Now, I live with a sense of freedom I never imagined having. God wants that for all of us. Sit back, relax, listen, apply action, and let us go on a journey that will change your life forever.

CHAPTER 1

KNOW WHO YOU ARE

When you know yourself, you are empowered.
When you accept yourself, you are invincible.

— Tina Lifford

Knowing who you are is the first thing you must know and understand. A lot of people think highly about somebody else's opinion, judgments, and labels. Disregard the opinions, judgments, and labels. The truth is you must know who you are and what God says about you. God says that we are made in His image. For all the people that look down on themselves and feel worthless, just know that you are created in God's image. You are created for a purpose, and knowing who you are will help to discover why you are here on earth. Negative things will form against you but will not prosper. This means that you will have trials and tribulations, but it will not overtake you.

Growing up in the church, I always felt that I had to experience the bad before I could have the good. I expected the negative first. I received the thing that I expected and wondered why these things were happening to me. In 1 Peter 2:9 KJV, God says that *"Ye are a chosen generation, a royal priesthood, a holy nation, a peculiar people; that ye should shew forth the praises of him who hath called you out of darkness into his marvelous light."* Why allow other people to call you the bad, disrespectful, uneducated, and unloving generation. At that moment, you should pull from within and see all the positive things about you and your generation. I have been told that you have a negative side and a positive side. The question was asked, "which one wins?" and the answer was the one you feed the most. What are you feeding yourself, and how do you feed yourself? What do you watch on TV, what kind of music do you listen to, what kind of conversations do you have on the phone, what kind of conversations do you have in your mind, and what kind of words do you speak out of your mouth? All these things do matter when you are trying to manifest something great in your life. For example, if you sit and listen to words and vibrations of a song that talks about nothing but negative things, then you will receive negative things. You are letting out levels of negativity into your current atmosphere. Let me be the first to say that all music is not negative. Some rap, country, R&B music is not all bad.

Scenario:

Tonya used to get in trouble at school through the years. She started trying to live a better life. She was tired of getting in trouble. Every year, the prior teacher would tell next year's teacher that Tonya is bad and that they needed to watch out for Tonya. Well, the receiving teacher already had preconceived ideas about Tonya. No matter how good Tonya tried to be, the receiving teacher could not see any good in Tonya. She allowed all the negative talk to cloud her mind about Tonya. She would accuse Tonya of doing things that she did not do. Tonya felt defeated and started doing the things that she was accused of doing. Tonya started lying, talking in class, not finishing her work on time, and disrupting the class. Tonya allowed the teacher to define her instead of being who she decided to be that year. The moral of the story is that Tonya wanted to change and show her positive side. Instead, she allowed the teacher's behavior to define her rather than be who she knew she could be, which was her true positive side. Tonya should have stayed focused on the positive instead of focusing on the teacher's behavior. It has been said what you focus on, you manifest. Through this experience, I vowed to do the following exercise, and it has forever changed my life.

Exercise:

Today, when you approach the world, it does not matter who it is that might try to define you, focus on who you are, or the person that you want to become, and your positive side will help you to overcome. Every time your negative side tries to take over your mind, repeat the affirmation throughout the day, and you will overcome it.

Affirmation:

I know who I am - I am focused, positive energy

Challenge:

I challenge you to practice the exercise 5 days in a row and monitor your progress. For a deeper experience, refer to the workbook.

CHAPTER 2

ONCE YOU BELIEVE IT – YOU OWN IT

Positive belief in yourself will give you the energy needed to conquer the world, and this belief is the power behind all creation.

— Stephen Richards

What do you honestly believe about yourself? Where does your belief system come from? Do you believe in yourself, or do you believe what other people say about you? Is your belief system causing you to be defeated or victorious in life? According to the dictionary, belief is when you accept that a statement is true or that something exists. Beliefs come from what we hear and keep hearing in our lifetime. Whether it is from our mothers' wounds , family members, neighbors, teachers, church members, store clerks, significant others, co-workers, newscast, TV, music, and others in passing, beliefs are being formed. Beliefs are also formed by our experiences, but mostly from believing what others say about us, and what we accept as true.

Anyone can say anything about you, but it does not mean anything until you believe it. Mark 11:24 says, *"Therefore I say unto you, What things soever ye desire, when ye pray, believe that ye receive them, and ye shall have them."* (KJV) The keyword in the above scripture is to believe that ye receive them and ye shall have them. Let's develop this a little further. The words that you hear, speak, read, or think become a part of your life if you hear them repeatedly. When you hear, your ears are listening, when you speak, your ears are listening, when you read, your ears are listening, and when you think, your ears are listening. Words are like seeds, the more you water them, the more they grow. As the words grow, they become a part of your belief system. Therefore, it is so important not to say negative things to your kids when you are mad because it becomes a part of what they believe about themselves. I know what you are thinking. You are thinking that one negative word or a few words are not going to hurt them. Let's suppose you get mad and say things that you do not really mean. The person that you spoke the negative words to takes them, internalizes them, and repeats them to himself or herself repeatedly. You have just caused them to form a belief about themselves that is surrounded around the negative words that you spoke. Then that person starts feeling sorry for themselves. A week later, things start going downhill for that person and you wonder what could be going on with them. They are still carrying those negative words around with them that you bestowed upon them because you did not control your anger. Here it is, you think everything is fine because you are not mad anymore. I always wondered why people often speak about ending their lives. Do not be the reason another person does not want to live because you cannot control your mouth. Believe it or not, this is one way that a person's belief system is created. Some people sit back and say things like, "I don't know where they get their ways from because my parents did not raise me like that." Your parents also did not speak negative things to you because they were angry. They believed in you and expressed it, and maybe this is the reason that you excel over others due to your level of positivity. Belief is another word for Faith. Everyone has Faith in something. Romans 10:17 KJV says that faith cometh by hearing, and hearing by the word of God.

You can have Faith negatively or positively; the choice is yours. You are free to make whatever choice you want to make, but you are not free from the consequences of that choice. Instead of playing the negative words over and over about what was spoken to you out of anger, turn the words around. If they call you stupid, pretend that they said that you were smart. Then declare and decree it over and over again until the negative words are out of your head. Do not allow someone else's negative words to define who you are and control what you believe.

"Belief is the source of your perspective which, in return, creates your reality."

— Demond Walker.

Scenario:

Tonya worked at a job where she had to meet with several of her co-workers. She was in a controlled environment and had no choice but to listen to the words that came from the other co-workers. Most of the time, it was extremely negative, and they often tried to say negative things about her indirectly. It was not because she did anything to them, it was because she was outdoing them, and she was new to the department. Every meeting, they would try to make her believe negative things about herself through their words. Little did they know, she left the meetings more encouraged than before she went into them. I know what you are thinking: how is that possible? Every time they spoke negative words, she simply wrote on her notepad the opposite over and over again. If they said that she was a cheater, then she simply wrote the following words: I am a winner. I am a winner. I am a winner. The more negative they spoke, the more positive she wrote. The positive words lifted her so high that she honestly believed that she was a winner.

Exercise:

When you are forced to be in an environment and must listen to other people's words, change them around by writing the positive version down. Repeat them in your mind until the negative words are gone.

Affirmation:

I believe that I am smart and sharp.

Challenge:

I challenge you to practice the exercise for the next 5 meetings and monitor your progress. For a deeper experience, refer to the workbook.

CHAPTER 3

KNOWLEDGE VS. LACK OF KNOWLEDGE

A lack of knowledge creates fear. Seeking knowledge creates courage.

— Candice Wanepoel

What is knowledge? The dictionary says that knowledge is facts, information, and skills acquired by a person through experience or education. Hosea 4:6, KJV says, God's people are destroyed from a lack of knowledge. You are not destroyed by the devil; you simply lack the knowledge in that area. Whatever area that you are failing in is a direct indication that you lack knowledge. It does not mean that you are stupid or lack the ability to do the task at hand. Some people look at others and think that they are just so smart while looking at themselves thinking and feeling like they are dumb. What those people fail to realize is the person that appears to be so smart took the time to obtain knowledge in that area, and it paid off. If there is anything in life that you are failing, take the time and obtain knowledge. Once you obtain the knowledge, you will become great at the very thing you seem to be failing. How do you obtain knowledge? Obtaining knowledge through research, mentorship, watching other people, and studying will help you to become successful in the desired area. Think about the knowledge you have in the areas where you are killing it. You had to do it over and over again until it became second nature. Remember when you were young and learned how to ride a bike? You were given the knowledge by whoever was teaching you on the do's and don'ts.

Then the person training you took the time to teach you how to use the knowledge given. Every day, when you got out of school, you were so excited to get on that bike to practice because you were getting better and better by the day. The more you rode the bike, the better you got until it became second nature to you. When you obtain knowledge and do not do anything with it – it becomes information. There is no reason to walk around feeling defeated in any area of life when there is so much knowledge available to you. Always put action into the knowledge that you gain. Knowledge gives you the power to overcome areas that need attention in your life. I know you have heard the phrase "knowledge is power." If you are powerless and need more power, you should gain more knowledge. Once you gain the knowledge, you must turn it into action. Then repeat the action over and over until you have mastered that area of your life. After you have absorbed the knowledge, it must be put into action, or it will go to waste. How do you turn knowledge into action? By taking what you have learned through your own experiences, books that you read, lectures that you have attended, through other people's experiences, and have the ability to turn it into action. Sharing knowledge will allow you to further absorb it.

Find ways to incorporate this into your daily routines and practices. Create a journal and write down what you learned. Some people have a hard time absorbing knowledge. In that case, you may have to read it several times before it sinks in. Then write it down repeatedly until it gets within you. Once you obtain the knowledge, no one can take it from you. It is yours for as long as you put it into practice. I have been told if you do not use it then it is a possibility that you might lose it.

In some cases, the knowledge that you obtain will become like second nature, and in other cases, you could lose it if you do not use it. God-given talents cannot be lost, but the skills that you have accrued can be lost if not used. Always remember that you cannot grow past your level of knowledge. How can someone help you if their knowledge level has not reached the level that you are on at that moment? Some arguments should have never happened because you are trying to make someone understand how you feel, and they lack the knowledge in that area. They cannot even comprehend what you are trying to describe. Therefore, you have been told to talk to someone that has gone through it successfully about your problems. You choose to turn to someone that cannot help you due to the lack of knowledge because they are your friend. You get mad because they do not understand what you are trying to convey. It is a clear indication that they have not obtained the level of knowledge that you are looking for at that time. When you notice that they just do not get it, just simply say okay, and change the subject. Find someone that has gone through the same thing successfully, can help you to understand, and can give you the knowledge that you so desperately need to make it to the next level in life. You can never rise above your level of knowledge, no matter how hard you try. Moving forward, when you are going through something for the first time or need additional help in an area, seek the knowledge. Luke 11:9 says, *"And I say unto you, Ask, and it shall be given you; seek, and ye shall find; knock, and it shall be opened unto you."*

Scenario:

I know someone can relate to this scenario. I wanted to go to this Law School that would allow you to work and go to school on the weekend. I talked to a couple of people that were from the area about the school. I started to get reports that the school was not accredited and that I would not be able to sit for the bar after completion. I realized later that I asked people that never attended the school. They discouraged me from going because of the knowledge that they obtained about the school. Years later, I found out that the knowledge given by the people that discouraged me was false. They gave me the knowledge that they had at that time. I should have done the research by talking to the ones that run the school or students that were attending the school. I did not do the research to obtain the knowledge that I needed to make an honest decision; therefore, I missed my opportunity. It was years later that I ran into someone that was going to the school that let me know that my information was incorrect. I could not get mad at the people that told me the prior information because they only gave me the knowledge they had about the school. When I think back on it, I could have graduated and be practicing law right now. When you do not seek the proper knowledge, it can really cost you dearly.

Exercise:

When you are seeking knowledge on something that you are trying to obtain, ask someone with the proper knowledge. Do the research, and you will be amazed as to what you find out in the process.

Affirmation:

I seek knowledge and find it daily.

Challenge:

I challenge you to practice the exercise for the next week and monitor your progress. For a deeper experience, refer to the workbook.

CHAPTER 4

FOCUS AND WORK ON YOU

Self-talk is the most powerful form of communication because it either empowers you or it defeats you.

— Noliana Chendang

Roman 4:17 says, *"Call those things that be not as though they were."* How do you call those things that be not as though they were? It is called Faith. Hebrews 11:1 says that now Faith is the substance of things hoped for, the evidence of things not seen. When God created the earth, He spoke it into existence. According to Genesis 1:3, God said, *"Let there be light: and there was light."* Pay attention to the word God said in the scripture above. Speaking things into existence is something that has been done daily whether a person knows it or not. I have so much to say in this chapter on working on yourself by speaking positive words over your own life. Some people speak positively over their life and negative over other people's lives. Well, they have just sowed a seed that will end up showing back up in their own life. If everyone understood that speaking bad or negative about someone else is like speaking over their own life, they would cease to speak that way about another. The more they speak negative or bad over someone, the more they are watering the seed. Words are like seeds. The more you speak them, the deeper they go and the more they grow. Some people feel that if they are just listening to a person talk about another person, then they would be fine. After all, it was not them talking as they were just listening. And that is where they are wrong. Let me explain. In Matthew 18:19, it says, *"Again I say unto you, That if two of you shall agree on Earth as touching anything that they shall ask, it shall be done for them of my Father, which is in heaven."* The moment you start listening to someone negatively talk about another person, and say, I hear you, or I understand, you have just put yourself in agreement with that person. Now that you agree, whatever that person talking negatively about belongs to you as well. Be careful what you listen to and who you agree to with over someone else's life. You are not focused on your own life and hurting yourself in the process. Do not sow negative seeds in somebody constantly and expect positive on your own life. We all know that the Bible says that you will reap what you sow. Sometimes it is more about what you are sowing in someone else's life. If you sow good, good will come back. If you sow bad, bad will come back. Often people will say "what did I do to deserve this in my life?" as they have forgotten about all the things that they spoke about somebody else's life. The reason they forgot about it is because it did not affect them directly. You must know that you cannot reap where you have not sown. If you do not like what you are reaping, change what you are sowing. Joel 3:10 says, *"Let the weak say, I am strong."* Take the things God says about you and implement them in your life and other people's lives. Job 22:28 says, *"Thou shalt also decree a thing, and it shall be established unto thee: and the light shall shine upon thy ways."* How do you declare a thing? You can decree and declare by speaking words and things into existence. Please refer to the scripture in Genesis, where God spoke the world into existence. Work on yourself by speaking things into existence in your own life.

Focus on you and not what others do or do not do. Begin changing your words to help build and edify yourself and others. I know you feel that I am focusing only on what you say about others. I want you to understand that the seeds, words, and thoughts that you speak about someone else are seeds that are accredited to you for the reaping. Begin today, speaking positive words like: "*I am the redeemed of the Lord and I say so, I am blessed and highly favored, I am accepted, I am chosen, I am loved, I am above only and not beneath, and I am the head and not the tail*". Begin to declare, decree, and affirm these things about yourself and others let the world know "this is who I am." Moving forward, you should get up every day and say, "*This is who I am.*"

Scenario:

Tonya was working at a job that required much focus. It was tough to get into the industry of adjusting. She started out knowing nothing about adjusting. She just remembers hearing all the rumors about how hard it was to survive your first deployment. She knew if she was going to survive that she needed to focus on herself and the job at hand. Every day, she would say things like, "*I can, and I will. I can do all things through Christ that strengthen me, this is easy, I am in it to win it, and I won't stop until I finish it.*" Tonya had to speak those things every day until they became a reality. Oftentimes, other adjusters that started out with her would come around so discouraged to the point they wanted to quit. She spoke positively over their lives because she knew it was like speaking it over her own life. She sowed positive seeds in other adjusters' lives and in her own life. Before you knew it, she had succeeded just by speaking positive words over her life and others' lives. She was at the end of the deployment as a new adjuster and made it to the next level. She made it past people that had been there a year or more. I genuinely believe it was all due to staying focused on herself and speaking positively over herself and others.

Exercise:

Every day, begin to declare and decree positive words over yourself and others. Every time something negative is presented, cancel it out with positive words.

Affirmation:

I am an overcomer. I am a peacemaker. I am lovable.

Challenge:

I challenge you to practice the exercise for the next week and monitor your progress. For a deeper experience, refer to the workbook.

CHAPTER 5

CREATE LIFE ON YOUR JOURNEY

Not everyone will understand your journey. That's ok.
You're here to live your life, not to make everyone understand.

— Tara Tierney

Creating life on your journey is something people pick up and put down. It is these types of attitudes that keep people going around in the circle of life. They feel good for a moment and then bad the next moment. They end up flashbacking and U-turning back to the life that they were living. They look up and ask the question: "How did I get back here?" What if I told you that it does not have to be like that? Whether you realize it or not, you are creating a life for yourself. You must understand that, every day that you get up, there are several paths that you can take. The choice is yours, but you are not free from the consequences of that choice. You are on a journey. Which way are you going to go on the path of life? You create your own life by the things that you desire, the words that you speak, the things that you listen to, the things that you see, the thoughts that you think, the things that you talk about out, and the things that you allow in your atmosphere. This is creating a life for you and your journey. Just like going down a road, you have a path where you go down one street, or you can go down the other street. It is a choice. Your path is created by the decisions that you make, and also the energy that you surrounds yourself with on your journey. The people that you surround yourself with make a huge impact on which way you travel and how far you go. When you think about it, it is simple. If you surround yourself with negative people, you will have a negative journey. If you surround yourself with positive people, you will have a positive journey. If you surround yourself with people that do not have anything to bring to the table, you will have a poor journey. If you surround yourself with people that know more than you, you will have a knowledgeable journey. I think you get the picture. You can create whatever journey you want in life but remember to go down the path that will take you higher. Every day you wake up, you are choosing your own path. Some people choose to work. Others do not. Some people choose to work for themselves, others do not, and some people choose to chill every day and depend on other people, others do not. The keyword here is choosing. It is simply your choice. Deuteronomy 30:19 says that God has set before you life and death, blessing, and cursing; therefore, choose life that both thou and thy seed may live. The good thing about choice is that you are doing the choosing, so if you are going down the wrong road, you can simply turn around and go down the right road. I have heard people say, "Well I missed my turn, so I will just stay on this path." If you miss it or blow it, just get up, turn around, and start again. Just because you fall or miss it, should not be an excuse just to stay there. You have not utterly failed until you quit. I do not know about you, but failure is not an option to choose. Never allow anyone to make you feel stuck by speaking negative things over your journey. I have heard people say that you are never going to be anything. "You are never going to do right." "I hate I even had you as a child." "You are an embarrassment to this family, and you are never going to amount to anything." If you allow those words to burn into your mind and soul or attach a belief to those words, your journey will be hard. You will have more success on your journey if you get up and prepare for it. Get up, talk to yourself, encourage yourself, get yourself a theme song, declare affirmations over your journey, keep positive energy around your journey, and show gratitude on your journey.

Let the world know that you are not a statistic, a punching bag, worthless, powerless, or stupid. Stand up, let the world know that you are created for greatness. I can, I will, and I am going to show you. Tonya, how do I know that I am on the right path? You know that you are on the right path when you step into new territory, when you are learning something new every day, and you look up to see that the people in your circle have changed.

Scenario:

When I started this job, it was very intimidating because everybody always talked about how hard it was to accomplish. I heard it was a hard job from everybody across the board. Before I started the job, I would affirm every morning. I am going to win. I begin telling myself. I am the best inside and outside of the building. I started to speak those things daily. The more I spoke it, the more I believed it. I began to listen to myself. My mind frame was so positive due to the affirmations that I spoke daily. It built confidence in me, and I really believed that I was a winner. My co-workers were saying that it seemed so easy for me and that I was catching on so fast. They asked me, "How do you do it?" I explained that I remain positive and speak positive affirmations over my life before I come into the building. They were looking at me saying, "She is lying, it has to be more than just that." They said to themselves, "This is so hard. I can't get this. I can't do this. What they did was create a life of failure around their journey for themselves, and I created a life of success around my journey. They created a hard journey because they kept looking at everything as being extremely hard. Because they focused on the negative, their attitude led them down the path to a defeated journey.

On the other hand, I was stress-free and was enjoying the job. I had a positive mindset on my journey. They had a negative mindset on their journey. It was easy for me because I created my journey around positivity and success. Are you creating hardship around your journey by speaking negative, or are you creating success on your journey by speaking positive?

Exercise:

Every day, begin to send positive affirmations ahead of difficult situations before you travel the path.

Affirmation:

I am always on the right path at the right time.

Challenge:

I challenge you to practice the exercise for the next couple of difficult tasks and monitor your progress. For a deeper experience, refer to the workbook.

CHAPTER 6

EVERYTHING THAT YOU NEED IS ALREADY MADE AVAILABLE TO YOU

Everything you need is already within you. The beauty of life is that your DESTINY lies always in your hands. The time has come for you to STEP UP and BE GREAT

— Pablo

I used to sit back and think, "Oh man, I want to be just like this person as they have it all together; this person has this and this person has that." Then I would look at another person and think, "Wow, this person has this, this person has that", and I would always sit back and feel like I wanted to be like them. I would always say, "Why can't I be like this, why can't I be like that?", not knowing the whole time that I already had it. When I began to get around these people, I began to think and say to myself, "What was I thinking? I do not like what I am experiencing when I get around these people." Everything that I thought I wanted turned out to be the very thing that I did not want. Exodus 20:17 says, *"Thou shalt not covet thy neighbor's house."* You know how it is when you want to be like other people because of what their life appears to be at that moment. Once you get in with those people, you become disappointed. You realize the person you thought they were turned out to be a fluke.

At some point in my life, I started asking God how I can do better in my own life. How can I be a positive force in the world? I asked God to place people around me that can help me. I read *As a Man Thinketh* by James Allen, *Power of Awareness* by Neville Goddard, and *The Charge* by Brendon Burchard. It was revealed to me that the authors had become my friends and my support system. Your friends, crowds, support systems, and mentors can be authors. It simply takes away the excuse that you do not have anyone. Some people do not have anyone, but you can pick up a book and read to stay in a positive environment.

I know some of you all think that I am going overboard. Let's look at this a little closer. Reading can be therapeutic, calming, vocabulary expansion, knowledgeable, peaceful, great mental stimulation, improved focus and concentration. Which would you rather have: a negative environment where you are always trying to make people understand you or read books that give you a positive vibe and positive influence? Reading helps you to see that everything that you have been looking for is already on the inside of you, just ready to be awakened. In the book Power of Awareness, Neville says, "because the inner you are molded in harmony with the sum total of all your beliefs, you will continue to have visible proof of the truth of that belief. For you will find millions believing with you, and you will believe that the numbers make it right, and so you will contribute to the whole vast traditions of men."

Reading will expose you to new beliefs and make you aware of what is on the inside of you. Growing up in the church allowed me to get the Word in me. Everything that I learn becomes real to me, the more I seek. I discovered that everything I needed was already within me. Here it is: I spent years looking for the right mentor, right church member, right friend, the right situation, and right moment thinking that those things would make me a better person. There is nothing wrong with mentors, great friends, or dedicated church members. If you were blessed to have those types of people in your life and they made a difference, that is a great thing for you. But what about the ones that did not have anyone no matter how hard they tried? The ones that trusted the people mentioned above but who molested them, set them up for failure, and talked down on them despite the positive changes that they were trying to make. I guess what I am trying to say: if you have been seeking for an outlet, look within. Just know that you no longer have to go without because some people refuse to let your past be the past, refuse to see the good in you, refuse to forgive you, refuse to love you through the hard times, or refuse to accept you for who you are. Learn to let it go, forgive, and move on. Stop allowing some people to bring you back to a place where you do not want to be because they are not ready for the positive you. What you need is already inside of you and is waiting to come out. You tap into it through faith. If you do not know where to start, read a book on the area of concern, or simply ask the question "Where I should start?" The answer will come and appear somewhere on your path.

Scenario:

When I started my journey of positive living, (not perfect living, there is a difference) I was hearing stories about this great life that I could have as it was made available to me. My current level of life was not helping me to get the things that God said that were mine for the taking. I remember looking around and thinking that God said that He owns the cattle upon the hill. God said that by His stripes, we are healed. I asked the question, "If these things are true, then why are so many people broke and sick? I began seeking God through prayer for the answer. He revealed to me that those people do not believe His Word and have not renewed their minds to the Word of God. Their mind is on the things that they deal with on a daily basis. I asked God to show me in my own life where I am not trusting in His Word and not renewing my mind. From that day to this day, I have been on a journey. On my journey, I would speak a positive affirmation and before the next sentence, I would finish it with a negative statement. I canceled my positive affirmation with a negative statement and wondered why I did not get the thing I affirmed. It was because I did not genuinely believe what I was affirming. Even after the negative statements would come, it was not until I continued affirming positivity that the negative words became less and less. It got to the point that I affirmed positivity over my life so much that I started to believe it. Once I believed, it was mine for the taking. I know some of you all are thinking this is just talk to put in the book. Let me ask you this: if someone can speak negatively so much that a person starts to believe the negative, then why it cannot work for positive as well? The moral of the story is to start right where you are and affirm the best until you see the best.

Exercise:

Start where you are today, affirm the best until you can start seeing a better way. Celebrate the small changes until they develop into big changes.

Affirmation:

Everything that I need is already made available to me under grace in a perfect way.

Challenge:

I challenge you to practice the exercise; start small and monitor your progress. For a deeper experience, refer to the workbook

CHAPTER 7

HOW PEOPLE TRIED TO DEFINE ME - PART 1

Be who you are and say what you feel, because those who mind don't matter, and those who matter don't mind.

— Bernard M. Baruch

I broke this title into several chapters because so many different people tried to define me. Where do I start, with so much to tell in a few paragraphs? Now that I know when someone is trying to define me, I can take it all the way back to childhood. I recall being at my cousin's house when we were younger, and her dad used to think that the other kids were the ones being bad. Little did he know or even care at the time, it was his own daughter that was leading the kids down the road of destruction. She would try to fight us and then play the victim after we fought her back. Her dad would call our mom and be like, "I am going to whip your kids if they fight my daughter again". He would say things like, "Your kids are bad", just to defend his own daughter. After growing into an adult, you can clearly tell who really picked the fights. My cousin's father tried to define me by saying that I was bad when I was defending myself. I had neighbors that tried to define me by saying all kinds of ugly things about me. No matter what I did for them, they could never see me as anyone other than what they said about me. They tried to make me believe that I was messy when in truth their life surrounded the mess. Over time, everything they said about my life became true in their own life. Lesson learned: do not try to make others look bad, because everyone will have their day where the seeds that were sown will sprout. My neighbors tried to define me as they were only interested in seeing the negative so that they could have something to talk about during their gatherings. Truth moment: I allowed what other people's expectations of me to grow inside. As a teenager, I was bad, fought often, picked at others, bullied people, and was disrespectful at times. When I did want to do the right thing, I had no one to turn to that could encourage me, as my circle could only see the negative side. It was still not who I really was, but who I allowed myself to become.

My mom would often tell me that she would not pat us on the back for something that we should be doing. Believe it or not, that made me stronger. I started seeing myself for who I really was and not how others viewed me. Their perspective of me was not my reality. I later learned that they could only see me as they see themselves. Thanks to my neighbors because, if it were not for them trying to define me, I would never have discovered who I really am today. Take a few minutes and reflect on the times someone tried to define you. My mom taught and instilled morals and values in me early in life. It was not until later in my latter years that I was able to pick up those attributes that my mom taught me and benefit from them. I had a good mother but she could not seem to let the past be the past. She always taught me to do the right thing, no matter what. When I became an adult, she would still identify me as that angry little girl. She often tried to define me from things that I used to do when I was a child. She just could not seem to let it go. Again, trying to define me. No matter what I did as an adult, she called me the same names that she called me as a child. Could it be the things that she wanted to see in me were already there, but her expectations were the same as when I was a child? The only good thing she would say about me was that I am a good mother to my children. I am an adult now, and I am just simply not the same anymore. Because she is my mother, should I have allowed her to continue to define me because I did not want to hurt her feelings? To keep from hurting my mother, could I have hurt myself? I got to the point that every time she tried to identify me as that child I once was, I would reply, "Thank you, Mother, my mother just said that I am the greatest." Or I would reply, "Thanks, Mom so are you," as if we were having a conversation. How many people out there have someone that refuses to see you for who you are now and not identify with who you used to be? It is called defining you. Try this, the next time that a person tries to define you, every time they speak something negative to you or about you, just turn and say, "*I cannot allow you to define me any longer. I am successful. I am beautiful. I am unique. I am peaceful. I am loved. I am purpose-driven, I am focused, and I am a positive force.*" By the time you finish, they will be gone. If they continue, repeat the above sentences. The negative does not like the positive.

Scenario:

When I was 13 years old, my auntie started taking me to church over in Mobile, Alabama. It is where I received my foundation. Now, before that, my mother always taught me right is right and wrong is wrong. But going over to Living Word Christian Center is where I started identifying with the person within. I learned the role and why I was here on earth. We sang songs that taught us how to worship God. I really learned the Bible scriptures due to the Word of God being preached so much during every type of service offered. For some odd reason, we stopped going to church, but I continued my journey. When I turned 18 years, I was able to drive myself, so I started going back to church. I learned so much as a young person. Our Bishop took a lot of time out with us, showing and teaching us who we were in Christ through his Word. We learned that we were valuable and set apart for God's purpose. I was seeking God on my own as I was hungry and wanted to know more. Once I found out that I was accepted by the beloved, from that day to this day, I have never tried to get anyone to accept me as I was already accepted. What a relief. I did not have to do drugs to be accepted, have sex to be accepted, steal to be accepted, lie to be accepted, cheat to be accepted, or drink alcohol to be accepted. So many people are caught up doing all sorts of things just to be accepted only to find out that it was not worth it. All those scriptures I learned started coming alive in me. I never relied just on the church service, I would ask the question, "What did I get out of the service today? How can I apply the scriptures to my life?" I was very dependent on God. I said, "Okay, Lord, whatever it is that you want me to do and whatever it is that you have for me, I pray that you show it to me." I allowed God to define me and vowed not to allow anyone else to define me. I had to renew my mind to the Word of God. The moment I stopped renewing my mind, I was attacked by someone trying to define me again. I would go back to God's Word to see what He said about me to counteract the definition. It became a way of life for me, and this is how You Don't Define Me came to life.

Exercise:

When people try to define who you like they know you better than you know yourself, renew your mind and refuse to let them define you.

Affirmation:

I have the mind of Christ. I am the redeemed of the Lord, and I say so.

Challenge:

I challenge you to practice the exercise often and renew your mind. Once you renew your mind, it will be hard to allow someone to define you. For a deeper experience, refer to the workbook.

CHAPTER 8

HOW PEOPLE TRIED TO DEFINE ME - PART 2

To be yourself in a world that is constantly trying to make you something else is the greatest accomplishment.

— Ralph Waldo Emerson

Let us talk about more situations where people tried to define me. This is a real experience that I had when this lady tried to define me. Not trying to expose anyone, I will use characters in this section. These characters are used just to help you understand this section. Let me tell you about what happened to me at a time in my life. Exposing the church or ministry is not necessary, as this is only designed to teach you about not allowing people to define you. What I am doing is exposing the spirit, and sometimes you must tell the story to reveal it.

Paula was always taught that every member should do their part in a ministry. She got involved with the street ministry. The street ministry was open to people that were coming off the streets and just needed help with food and clothes. Paula loved helping people, so this was a good fit. The first day serving, it felt like a mini church service. Sally would pray, teach Word, and the rest of the time left was used to clean up the area. Paula was trying not to judge, but after about 3 meetings, it was getting hard to sit there through hours of preaching about how God allowed curses on people because they did not do the things she asked them to do. Paula wanted to leave, but she stuck it out. She said, "I'm going to give this an honest attempt and just try to remain focused." Sally did some things that Paula did not like—first, she talked about a person that was supposed to be her assistant. Paula was not sure if Sally was trying to mention things about her assistant to be prayerful or messy. Paula was new to the Street ministry and did not know what to think. Paula thought to herself, "Okay, nobody is perfect, but this is just not something that I want to be bothered with." Paula said that something just did not feel right. At this point in Paula's life, she would never be bothered by this type of behavior on the streets, and she certainly did not want to be bothered in the church. Sally started talking about people in different parts of the ministry, and Paula knew this was some type of mess. Although Paula wanted to quit, she stuck with the task at hand. Normally, if this type of behavior were happening in the streets, Paula would have left. Why did she stay? I guess she felt that it would be a disappointment to God. A couple weeks later, the assistant left, and Paula started assisting Sally. She called Paula on her cell phone and started gossiping. Paula was shocked and explained to Sally that she did not like talking on her personal cell phone and wanted to know if she could just talk to her in the office. Sally agreed.

One day Sally started preaching, and at the end, as always, Paula only had a small window to clean up. Apparently, it was some people at the front door that needed assistance. Paula was in the back cleaning when they were being served. Sally ran out in the middle of the building, yelling that people's lives were in the balance. She told everyone to put down there cleaning tools, stop, and pray. Everyone started praying. Sally said that people listen to the pastor, but not to the one he put in charge of the ministry. Paula thought to herself, "What is this lady talking about?" Paula started thinking that none of this is edifying or building her up. Sally picked up a bag of trash out of a small trash can and asked

Paula to take it outside. Paula thought that it was strange because, normally, the trash is taken to the back storage room. Well, when Paula came back in from outside, Sally did not know she was back. She was in another room talking to another one of the ladies that was helping as well. The lady was trying to nod her head to Sally to let her know that Paula came back in, but it was too late, she heard Sally say, "Did you see her, the way she was acting when I told you all to pray?" Paula thought to herself, "I'm not going to sit here and deal with any mess, I just refuse to, I do not care what part of the ministry it is coming from." Paula waited until the day was finished, pulled Sally to the side, and said, "Just want to let you know right now. I'm not going to be able to further commit to this part of the ministry." Sally was fine with it and said that she understood. Paula knew that God was not the author of confusion. Ministry versus mess, which one do you manifest?

After Paula released herself, she thought that it was all over. It was just the beginning. Sally pretended to be understanding. On her way home, Paula started getting calls and text messages, saying, "God is not through with you." "You are disobedient to God, and God is not through with you", and "You need to continue to do what God told you to do." After more text and calls saying words such as, "You need to do this..." and "You need to do that...." Paula thought to herself. "I'm just not going to be bothered with confusion." Paula was not going to allow Sally to define her by putting God's name before every sentence.

So, Paula continued to keep her position. Her position was, "Hey, I'm not going to do it." This did not stop Paula from visiting the church. One night, Paula and her sister went to the church, and Sally was preaching that night. The characters are not real, but this is a true story. Sally directed the whole service to Paula. She said during her sermon, "You need to come back and finish what the Lord gave you to do." Sally's entire message was about God not being done with Paula. Sally said, "You listen to the Pastor, but you do not listen to the one he put in charge." Do not allow people, situations, and circumstances to control or define you. Paula did not allow Sally to define her or control her at that time. Paula refused to have unforgiveness towards Sally for what she had done. So Paula said softly to herself, "I love, and I forgive you, I love, and I forgive you, I love, and I forgive you," until the spirit of unforgiveness left. Paula knew she had forgiven Sally when she saw her and able to hug her, not feeling resentment. Even if they are in the church, do not allow anyone to make you be a part of something that is not like Christ. The point is Sally is not perfect and, at some point, allowed gossiping to take over at that moment. Paula did not want to deal with that type of energy as she went there to help others. Sally tried to define Paula after she would not return to the street ministry. Paula knew that negative energy and allowing people to define her could have destroyed her own self-image. In some cases, people will try to define you by using God's name. This is one reason you must know God for yourself.

Scenario:

When Tonya was young, she wanted to get involved in the youth ministry. They were having an event for young people. The church was looking for volunteers and she said to them that she wanted to get involved. They told her to fill out the paperwork, then they would get back with her. She filled out the paperwork, turned it in, and waited next to the phone. She was extremely excited. She sat there with great anticipation. Days passed, and no one had called. Tonya thought to herself, "She said they would call me." Nobody got back with Tonya. Nobody said anything to her.

Then after church one day, she saw the person that was over the event and asked him again, "Hey, do not forget about me." He replied, "Oh, we will not. We'll never forget about you." Even after she reminded them, Tonya never received a call. The event had come and gone. She did not know if they forgot about her, if it was a disconnect, or what the reason was that they did not call. The next week, when Tonya went to church, the ministry leader said, "Hey, we did not see you at the event," Then I replied, "I never received the call." And she said, "They called." I replied, "I never received a call nor a voicemail." She said, "They were supposed to call you." I thought about the conversation in my head.

Tonya did not know if she was lying, or did somebody tell her that they called? Tonya did not know what happened that day, but she knew that she was not going to allow this situation to define her. I do not care if it is a pastor, a pastor's wife, a minister, a deacon, a musician, church member, co-worker, manager, leader, or a politician, never allow anyone to make you feel less than important. I do not know who you are; however, I do know who I am. I am not going to allow anybody to define my worth. Tonya still worked with youth in her city, made a difference, and enjoyed it. Just because someone does not acknowledge your gifts and talents, use them anyway. Find another way, just refuse to stop until you have reached the top.

In the first story, Paula was not able to use her talents and gifts in the street ministry due to Sally keeping up the mess. In the scenario, Tonya was not given a chance to use her talents and gifts due to suppression. Regardless, as to which situation you have encountered, never allow anyone to suppress your God given talent or define who you are.

Exercise:

When people do not acknowledge your gifts and talents, use them anyway. Find another avenue. Refuse to stop until you reach the top.

Affirmation:

I use my gifts and talents to build and edify. I believe in my skills and abilities.

Challenge:

I challenge you to practice the exercise. Add to your skills/talents until you master them. For a deeper experience, refer to the workbook.

CHAPTER 9

HOW PEOPLE TRIED TO DEFINE ME - PART 3

Follow your heart, listen to your inner voice, stop caring about what others think.

— Roy T. Bennett

When I was younger, I worked at Walmart. When working at Walmart, you were on a 90-day probation period before being offered a permanent position. After your 90-day probation, then you were considered full time or let go. So, on my 90-day probation, I was promoted to manager. My promotion did not sit well with other employees because I was young and was only there for 90 days. They were people that were there for a long time, and I guess they felt like it should have been them promoted over me. As a result, they tried to make my management experience a living hell. They were trying to talk about me, make it hard for me, and did not want to listen to me because they were twice my age. They tried to create a bad environment for me only because I was chosen over them. I thought to myself, "Okay, so I was chosen to be a manager, and I am going to show the world that I can do this well." One thing they could not deny is that I was good at what I did. I was one of the best cashiers and always was on the top of the list for the highest number of scans. They really could not stop me from doing the job itself because I knew how to do it. However, they just tried to make it hard for me by talking about me. They refused to do what was asked without giving me the third degree because they did not want to take directions from a young person and went so far as to lie to me. I thought to myself, now these women are two and three times older than me, so why would they act like that at this age?" I just could not believe it. I was shocked. Now, I do know that jealousy, envy, and strife could have played a role in their behavior. I know all those things do exist, but I was not going to allow it to define me. I decided that I was promoted to manage my shifts and that I would manage them to the best of my ability. To be honest, it was not easy at first. I had to encourage myself before going into the building. I had to consistently remind myself that I can, and I will. I somehow knew within that I was built for this and that I would make it no matter what I had to face. The managers that chose me believed I could do it, and I was not going to let them down or myself down. These experiences caused me to be tough and help prepare me for future jobs. There were days that I wanted to cry because, in my mind, I thought these women were supposed to teach me how to be a better person. As time passed, things got better and better. I came to realize that these women could not help me because they were ignorant. I turned my attention to the people that could help me, and I focused on that alone. I believe changing my focus caused me to have a better experience. The more I did not pay the pettiness any attention, the more it stopped. Looking back at it now, those women did not know how to deal with disappointment and took their problems out on me. I worked there for a good while, and I did what I had to do. I ran my shifts successfully. They did not run me off. They tried, but it did not work. It is funny how someone will try to define you because of a promotion that you had nothing to do with. Knowing that if they were chosen, they never would have treated me that way. I would like to thank those ladies because they taught me what not to do. They taught me not to pay attention to other people's pettiness. They taught me not to allow anyone else's jealous acts to define me. Remember to find ways to rise above it all, and you will not be disappointed. It has been said that if you are thrown lemons, make lemonade.

Scenario:

Betty worked for a company and had a Christian manager. Betty was a great worker, and her manager loved her work ethics. Betty was dependable, always showed up to work on time, had great customer service skills, was trustworthy, and got along well with others. Betty's manager said, "I just want to commend you on everything that you do because when you work, you work, you do things that I do not even ask you to do, and I just want to commend you." And Betty told her that the pastor taught them about never being a slave. The pastor said, "If you do not want to be a slave to anybody when they ask you to do something, always do one thing over, and you will never be a slave." The manager then replied, "You know what, I'm going to write your pastor a letter and let your pastor know he is doing a wonderful job with the young people." Betty started talking about going back to school to her manager because they would talk at times. The manager tried to discourage Betty from going back to school by asking, "What are you going to do? How are you going to do that?" And she was trying to intimidate Betty because she did not want her to leave the job. After all, Betty was a good worker, and she did not want to lose a good worker. We all have experienced times when someone did not want us to do something that we wanted to do. Betty decided not to allow the manager to define her, left the job, and went to school. If anyone tries to discourage you from doing better in life, get away from them immediately.

In the first story, I was exposed to older people that should have been trying to teach me how to excel in life but could not see past their own jealousy. They tried to define me by trying to make me quit and trying to define my future. In the scenario, Betty's manager tried to discourage her because she did not want to lose her as an employee. She tried to discourage her from furthering her education. She also was trying to define her future. No matter what, do not allow anyone to keep you from bettering yourself. Just let them know that you do not define me or my future.

Exercise:

If you are in a situation where a manager, teacher, trainer, or mentor is trying to discourage you, find a way to cut ties and move forward. Show them that you are created for greatness.

Affirmation:

I am created for greatness. I am an overachiever. I am the cream of the crop, and I rise to the top.

Challenge:

I challenge you to practice the exercise. Always strive to be better today than you were yesterday. For a deeper experience, refer to the workbook.

CHAPTER 10

HOW PEOPLE TRIED TO DEFINE ME - PART 4

Don't compromise yourself - you're all you have.

— John Grisham

Well, I left Walmart and went off to school. I attended the Montgomery Job Corps Center. Job Corps was a place where you could obtain a trade that offered the skills you needed for the workforce. My mindset was focused on doing things that I never did before. I was ready to try something different. When I arrived at school, everyone was amazing. This was the first time some people were away from home, and the staff tried to make everyone feel comfortable. The entire staff were great mentors. They were great people. They all had degrees and were very professional. I was so excited to be there as I realized that I was in new territory and ready to learn. I believed that I would do great things on this new journey. Everything inside of me just knew it to be true. Before attending the school, I was aware of who I was and had a solid foundation. I vowed that I would not let anybody turn me back to where I came from. I was ready for anything at this point. I had been building myself up through the scriptures. The trade that I was working on was clerical occupations at that time. They had different steps and levels in the programs that you could push yourself to obtain. The first year that I was there, I was summoned to be the secretary of the Student Government Association. The current secretary had to resign. I accepted the position as my trade was in clerical occupations, and I felt that it would only add value to my business skills. Well, I joined the group and enjoyed it. The SGA-advisor was exceptionally good, knowledgeable, and a great role model. All the staff were good role models. I was thankful as this was different than the older people at Walmart. My clerical teacher was knowledge-able, and she taught us the skills that were needed to run an office. She also taught us social skills. We had competitions in class, tying and ten-key competitions. Once I learned the skill, I made my way to the top of the list. Everyone that knows me understands that I love a good challenge. By being on the SGA, I had to work harder because I was out volunteering in the community and still had to complete my work. I was involved in so many activities and played active roles in several different areas on and off campus. They are as follows just to name a few: Hayneville Road Elementary School Big Buddy Program, Thanksgiving/Christmas Family Donation Program, Jump Rope for Hearts/Hoops for Hearts Program, UNCF Bowl-a-Thon Program, and passing out new bus route schedules in the community.

We did on-campus events. I was the canteen manager, where I had to make sure that all the food was ordered, kept up with the books, money, and reported it back to my SGA advisor. Being the canteen manager came naturally easy to me. I became an ambassador for new students that enrolled into Job Corps to assist them as needed. I was appointed to be the peer mediator judge along with other people assisting me on the board. When a student had a minor conduct offense, they had to appear before the peer mediator judge and argue their innocence to be reviewed. My board members and I would decide if the offense should stick or be removed. If it stuck, then we would decide the punishment. If it was removed, they were free to go. It was a great experience and was something that I never did before. I was quad vice president first and then became quad president. The quad was our living area, where we would have meetings to address issues in the dorm. I was the Cougar newspaper editor. I was the speaker that ran the awards ceremony alongside my advisor. The awards ceremony was done monthly. Every month, I received an award for student of the month in more than one of the following to name a few: Female Quad 1 Student of the Month, Best All-Around Student of the Month, Distinguished Leadership Award for the Month, Academic Student of the Month, and Trade Student of the Month, etc.

I am accustomed to winning. Everything I am involved in is a win for me. I am not in competition with anyone but myself to do better than I did the day before. We had a phase incentive, where the goal was to get from phase one to phase five. I was one of very few to make it to phase five and was able to maintain the phase once I reached it. I always had this winning attitude. It was my mentality and because of that, I achieved great results. As a result of the things that I accomplished, a few of my peers tried to attack my character. They did not like the attention and positive energy that surrounded my name. They set out to make it all unravel. They tried but failed. All the lies that were told, rumors that were spread, and false accusations faded by the day. No one believed them or paid any attention to them. After they realized that it did not bother me, they went on to the next person.

In this story, my peers were trying to define and/or confine me. The more I identified with the real me, the more of a stereotype they tried to put on me. The higher your success, the higher the attack. Even when you are living your best life, some people still try to define you. They so desperately want to confine you to control you. You Don't Define Me is not always about attacking the negative, sometimes it is about pushing forward to get to a higher level in life. Sometimes it is about breaking forth through other people's confinements.

Scenario:

Jessica attended Faulkner University and was doing quite well for herself. Once again, Jessica was in competition with herself trying to do better than she did the day before. She met a lady in her class named Tia. She wanted to be study partners with Jessica. They were in the same class that met on Tuesday night. Every week when the grades would come out, they both had rather good grades. A couple of weeks, Jessica did a little bit better than Tia. One Tuesday night, they were scheduled to take a quiz. Jessica expressed that she did not study well the following night. Tia offered to show Jessica her answers after she was done. Jessica declined, put her head down, and took her own test. Tia was sitting in front of Jessica and thought that she copied her answers. Tia started plowing the ground, trying to play innocent like she did not know all the tests were different. She told Jessica that she thinks it was a big mistake allowing her to copy the answers. Tia told Jessica that she thinks that the test may have been different. The next week the grades came out, and to Tia's surprise, Jessica aced the test. The moral of the story is that Jessica could not trust Tia after suggesting that she should cheat off her test. Tia tried to confine Jessica, or should I say, control her grade. Tia did not like Jessica excelling over her and tried to sabotage her grade on the quiz. Beware of people that appear to help you with unethical acts. What are they really trying to do?

Exercise:

If you are in a situation where someone is trying to confine or control you with unethical acts, do not trust them. Make every effort to triumphant over the area that they are trying to stop.

Affirmation:

I am triumphant, and I am victorious. I succeed over everything I touch.

Challenge:

I challenge you to practice the exercise. Always push past people's traps that are designed to hold you back in life. For a deeper experience, refer to the workbook.

CHAPTER 11

HOW PEOPLE TRIED TO DEFINE ME - PART 5

Don't compromise yourself - you're all you have.

— John Grisham

What is a lie? Lying is a form of deception. Lying is giving someone the wrong information knowing that it is not true, to deceive the one receiving the information. Some people will try to make you believe a lie about yourself in the hopes of defeating you. That is exactly what my opponent was trying to do to me. After being successful in my secretary role at Montgomery Job Corps, I decided to run for SGA president. In my campaign, I never said anything negative about my opponent. I focused on what I was going to do if chosen for the role. My opponent thought that, because she was a follower and did what others wanted her to do, it would help her to win. After all, I did not run with their cliques. I did not get involved in things they wanted me to get involved in. I encountered much opposition, but it comes with the territory. You must be willing and ready. I asked myself often, "Why am I here and have I accomplished what I came to do?" I stayed focused on why I was there, and it helped me tremendously. Anything a person said or did to me negatively, I ignored, as I was great at blocking it out. If I know that I have not done anything bad to a person that attacks me, I will not make time for that negativity in my life. Truth moment: Whatever issues they were having with me, they were going to work them out themselves. I did not even hang out with the negative crowd, and I was not going to get involved with their negative energy. I learned to activate the mind over matter skills. The dictionary states that mind over matter is used to describe a situation in which someone can control a physical condition. I had the strength to carry on to the finish line. They did not understand where I came from and what all I had been through prior. None of those things matter; if they were not positive, I did not engage at all. Through it all, I was able to remain free from all the drama. Part of the reason some people talked about me was because I refused to join their groups. Some of them thought that I was stuck up. Some did not like me because they did not like my advisor. Some were jealous, and some were just ignorant. More people liked me more than not. I just refused to allow any of them to define me on any level. Campaigning was over, and the speeches were given. The time was nigh for the voting to take place. To my opponent's surprise, I won by a landslide. She immediately demanded a recount. Regardless of how many times you recount the votes, I was still the new President of SGA.

I know that I make it appear to be easy, but some days it was hard. I tried my best to keep a positive mindset. I turned to my counselor, and she encouraged me to keep moving forward as it appeared that I was on the right track. Later, at the end, some of them apologized to me for going along with the foolishness. Truth moment: Now, while they were apologizing, I was like, "Oh, okay, I understand," but I was not paying much attention to them. I did not care about what they were doing, that was their business and not mine. I know that it may seem to be on a thin line of a proud spirit. Still, I was simply trying to remain focused and humble enough to accept their apology and not get caught up in their affairs. Now, I know nobody likes to be picked on, talked about, or bullied. When you are already accepted in the beloved, and you learn to love yourself, other people's opinions do not matter. I had way more good days, more good conversations, and more good things happened to me than bad. At this point in my life, I knew how to separate myself from the negativity, just like I knew how to create it, I knew how to separate myself from it as well. I learned so much about myself and another level of not allowing people to make me believe a lie about myself. If I had to do it all over again, I would do it in a heartbeat. I think that staying focused on the task at hand is what brought me the victory. Think about it; if I had my mind on what my opponent was doing, I would have been distracted and could have lost it all. Once you are distracted, you may never recover and lose the very thing you were trying to accomplish.

Scenario:

Renae entered a program called TCU advanced training program. The program was designed to prepare students that were interested in working at the train station. Renae rode the Marta train to get to school in downtown Atlanta, GA. Renae was excelling very well in the program; however, it was not what she wanted to continue to do. The vocational advisor got mad at Renae because she felt like she was doing such a great job. She advised Renae to stay and finish the program even though she did not have any interest in furthering her training. She reminded Renae about all the opportunities and benefits of the training. She tried to convince Renae to give it a couple more weeks, but Renae declined it. The advisor got so mad that she started telling the other students that Renae was stupid. One student came to Renae and asked her, "What is wrong with that advisor, that lady was saying that you were stupid for leaving a good program like TCU." According to that student, the advisor told her that she could tell Renae as she did not care. The advisor was trying to define Renae by calling her stupid. She wanted it to get back to Renae, and that was the reason she told the other students. Beware of people that tell other people things to report back to you, they are just trying to define you in hopes they get what they were looking for.

In the first story, I was determined to stay focused on what I was trying to accomplish and not on the lies or distractions that were designed to make me fail. I have been told that failure is only a broken focus. My opponent tried to define me by distractions and lies. In the scenario, the vocational advisor tried to define Renae through put-downs and gossip. Either way, do not fall for the traps set by people trying to define you for their own personal gain.

Exercise:

If you are in a situation where someone is trying to set traps for you to fail through put-downs or gossip, do not entertain it. Smile and keep going in the direction of your vision.

Affirmation:

I have an inner vision that is always clear, I am valuable.

Challenge:

I challenge you to practice the exercise. Stay focused and free of all indirectly sent distractions. For a deeper experience, refer to the workbook.

CHAPTER 12

HOW PEOPLE TRIED TO DEFINE ME - PART 6

Think for yourself, or others will think for you without thinking of you.

— Henry David Thoreau

Religious belief shapes people's morals, customs, traditions, and behavior. In most cases, shared religious beliefs bind people together. Lily meets a family that was religious while enrolled in school out of town. She was excited as she wanted to connect with like-minded people. Keep in mind, Lily has always been able to attend a church service and receive her portion. She has been taught that when you attend a church, you submit to the order of service. If it is something that does not agree in your spirit, then you probably should not be going to that service. One thing that Lily loved about this family is that they fellowshipped with one another weekly, monthly, and during holidays. In the beginning, it was a positive environment. The family sung worship songs, studied the bible, ate healthy food, prayed, and had good family fun together. It is what every person that is seeking God prays for often. When the weekend approached, we knew that it was going to be a good fellowship. Lily spent years with their family, fellowshipping and just enjoying one another. I know what you are thinking: "So what is the problem?" Everything was great until they started basically saying if you do not believe the way they believe then you are not doing what God wants you to do. Lily's thoughts were, "How do you know what God is telling me to do?" As the years went by,

Lily started noticing their behavior. Romans 3:23 says that all have sinned and come short of the glory of God. We know that no one is perfect, including Lily. They were blind to the things they did that were wrong. They could only see the other person's wrong. They would make comments like "God is not sleeping." This made Lily think, "Was God asleep when you stole from the salvation army, lied, tried to control people's actions through lies, conquered, and divided people?" They were nice, helpful, loving, and successful in some areas until you decided to go the way that you felt God was leading you to go. Once you wanted to live your own life, make your own mistakes, and make your own moves, you were considered sneaky, untrustworthy, and unholy. Truth moment: Lily's son was riding in the car on a cool sunny evening and made the following statement at 11 years old: "Mom, these people are always in church, the kids go to the church school, but they act nothing like Christ." Lily was shocked and could only tell her son that nobody is perfect.

Have you ever had a Christian to help you, bless you with things, and treat you with the love of God until you decide to know God for yourself? The moral of the story is some Christian's serve God so long, do not renew their mind, get stuck in their ways, think that they are the only ones right, feel that if you tell them no that God will try to punish you, or that God speaks to them only. Some Christians want to control you, but God gives you freedom of choice. Control is another form of defining. If you are this type of Christian, repent to God, renew your mind so that you do not keep defining people, let go and let God. Some people have been Christians for so long, they forgot about the things they went through and how they had people to pray for them through the tough times. Lily had high expectations for her weekend Christian family. She realized that they had been Christians for so long and forgot about their own trials and tribulations, they were not showing the love of God. They did several nice acts but were not able to show the love of God.

Lily recognized that no one is perfect, and she should never expect more from a person than God.

Scenario:

Kizzy went off to the military and met this lady named Minnie who worked for the military. Minnie knew that Kizzy had some issues but tried to just show the love of God by praying for her and inviting her to church. The day came that Minnie finally invited Kizzy to church, and she went. Kizzy came back to the base, amazed by the experience that took place in her life that night. She had an encounter with the Holy Spirit. Kizzy said that she was praising and worshipping God, started crying, and felt so much love. She was crying uncontrollably and knew that she was touched by the Spirit. From that day forward, Kizzy realized that God loved her despite the imperfections. The moral of the story is that Minnie knew that Kizzy had issues, did not try to solve them, control the situation, or try to define her. She simply showed the love of God and allowed the Spirit to work on Kizzy. In the first story, the Christians were nice and did nice acts. But they forgot about loving people versus trying to control or define them. In the scenario, Minnie did not try to change, control, or define Kizzy. She prayed for her and showed the love of God. We all, at some point in our walk, need to show more of God's love.

Exercise:

If you are in a situation where someone is trying to control or define you, seek God. Ask God to give you wisdom on how to handle the situation and pray for the individual. God is love. Let us practice walking more in the love of God this week by our actions.

Affirmation:

I am love, I am loved, I am lovable.

Challenge:

I challenge you to practice the exercise. When you see a person in need, stop and say a word of prayer. For a deeper experience, refer to the workbook.

CHAPTER 13

HOW PEOPLE TRIED TO DEFINE ME - PART 7

Never be bullied into silence. Never allow yourself to be made a victim.
Accept no one's definition of your life but define yourself.

— Harvey Fierstein

When Andrew first heard that his current employer was looking for people to join the adjusting field, he was ecstatic. He immediately let his current supervisor know that he was interested in becoming an adjuster. Andrew heard people in his current position tell horror stories about people that tried to be an adjuster. He was told about the ones that left for lunch and never returned. The ones that called into work sick for days due to being stressed. Even the ones that ran out just to burst into tears. Andrew knew that this would be particularly challenging, but he was up for the challenge. The first day he did on the job training, and the pressure was on. Let me explain that during job training, you sit with one person that is adjusting claims and you try to learn from them. Basically, you learn as you go. Andrew did not know what was more challenging, not knowing what to do and trying to figure it out or trying to sort through all the emails that were designed to help move him forward. Andrew knew that, if he was going to make it, he needed to get in a positive mind frame. He asked questions and could feel that his cubemate did not want to be bothered as she was trying to do her own work. He knew if he did not ask questions, he would not survive. He asked the cube-mate first, then the neighboring adjuster, then one of the trainers, then the other trainer, then adjusters on other rows until he found the answer. He asked so many questions, it got to the point where everyone put up a sticker on their cube that said, "no more Andrew lol." It paid off, after a month, Andrew was standing on his own two feet. He learned enough to excel, go to the next level, and was operating at a fast pace. Suddenly, he became the number one closer in the building. How can a person that did not know anything about adjusting rise to the top so quickly?

Andrew was all about the power of positivity. Before he started the day, he would affirm in the mirror that he could and would accomplish more today than he did yesterday. He played positive affirmations daily and let them play in the background as he was getting ready for work. He prayed and asked God for wisdom on how to accomplish his daily goals. He even went so far as to sing songs about how he would overcome that day successfully. I know that you are wondering how that is possible. Well, he would put on an instrumental song and add positive words to it. He customized the words to fit his current situation. I know some people may laugh, and some may think that it is to the extreme. 1 Corinthians 1:27 says, *"But God hath chosen the foolish things of the world to confound the wise; and God hath chosen the weak things of the world to confound the things which are mighty;"* Andrew made songs out of things he went through. His sister used to laugh at him until she started seeing the results of it, and then she said, "Well, you know what? I am going to start doing what Andrew is doing," because she wanted results in her own life. Andrew stated, "If I am feeling a type of way that is negative, I am making a positive song out of the situation. If I feel like somebody did me wrong or got wind of something negative, I am making a positive song out of it, and sing, 'It is in my favor. It is in my favor. It is in my favor.'" Andrew was not one to accept defeat. How was Andrew able to excel so much further than the other adjusters that came in with him? Positivity played a major role but was not the only reason. Andrew was focused and was not easily distracted. Some of his peers were discouraged, spoke defeat over their progress, and spoke negative words over themselves. Some adjusters felt like they were dumb, started saying that they would not make it, and they would probably be the first to get cut when it slows down. Please tell me who could make it through those types of defeated statements. Think about it: they are working hard, doing their best, and not getting far. Anyone would be frustrated with those types of results after working hard. They were doing it to themselves, they would speak negatively, join up with another adjuster that felt the same way, and both discuss all the things that went wrong. Andrew tried to encourage them, speak positive to them, and discuss the power of positivity. They thought that it had to be more and dismissed the power of positivity.

Scenario:

There was a young lady at one of the jobs that I worked in the past. I helped this young lady to succeed on the job, as she was not doing well. I wondered why she was not doing well; maybe because she was causing problems in other people's lives. I noticed how she would spread rumors and not know if they were true. Well, that was my exit. I do not mind helping you, but I am not going to hurt myself to help you. I was telling my sister and my baby cousins, if someone does things in front of you, they will do it to you. You are next in line. The problem is everybody thinks they are different and that person would never do it to them. Speaking negative, spreading lies, and spreading rumors is like releasing negative vibes on someone else's life. If they knew releasing negative over another person's life is like releasing it over their own life, they would think twice. Everyone is guilty of this at some point in life, but that is not an excuse to stay there. Rise up, speak up, look up, and together we can use our voice for the better good.

In the first story, Andrew was speaking positivity over his difficult situations. The more he spoke positively, the better it got. Other adjusters spoke defeat and it was reflected in their progress. Henry Ford said, "If you think you can, or if you think you can't, you are right." In the scenario, a co-worker was speaking negatively over everyone else and could not understand why it was so difficult for her to get ahead as she needed so much help. She probably should have used her voice to speak positive over someone else's life as it was just like speaking over her own life.

Exercise:

When you are around people who are trying to be optimistic and speak positive, join in with them. Let them know that you support what they are doing.

Affirmation:

I am supportive, I make a positive difference, I am connected to positive circles.

Challenge:

I challenge you to practice the exercise. When you see a person trying to be optimistic and find the positive, join in and make a difference. For a deeper experience, refer to the workbook.

CHAPTER 14

HOW PEOPLE TRIED TO DEFINE ME - PART 8

Keep your thoughts positive because your thoughts become your words. Keep your words positive because your words become your behavior. Keep your behavior positive because your behavior becomes your habits. Keep your habits positive because your habits become your values. Keep your values positive because your values become your destiny.

– Mahatma Gandhi

Alley: What does that quote have to do with managing?

Andre: It has everything to do with managing.

Alley: No one can be positive all the time with deadlines, emails, and responsibilities.

Andre: Keeping a positive mindset has nothing to do with completing tasks on the job. It is about having the right attitude.

Every company wants customers that are pleased and happy. The reason several companies have surveys is because they want to make sure that their customers are satisfied. The survey will allow the company to keep up with the employee's performance from a customer's point of view. With that in mind, if a manager has a nasty negative attitude, it will eventually rub off on the employees. For example, if you have a manager tell an employee that the customer's request has been denied in a nasty negative way, the employee may take that same energy back to the customer. A couple days later, a survey was completed by a customer, and the customer gave the employee a bad score. Now the employee has a negative customer review, further making the company look bad. Where did the negative energy originate? It originated from the manager. Now let us look at it from another point of view: the manager discusses all the options with the employee for the customer. With an open mind, they found options that were not there prior because of the mindset. A positive mind will create an atmosphere for an open mind. You will discover more solutions than problems. Now the employee goes back to the customer with a positive attitude and open mind. As a result, the company will have better customer satisfaction. Do you see the difference? The problem is that some managers do not have a positive mindset. Managers play a major role in the team's morale and daily results. If the manager is condescending, gossips about the team behind their back, cuts their own supervisor down in front of the team, tells lies on others to shift the blame, tries to control the team versus manage the team, micro-manages while looking for negativity, belittles the team because they do not have the answer, embarrasses the team, consistently criticizes the old and new processes, and does not show respect for the team, the team will have a hard time going to the next level. You know what I am talking about, we all had or knew a manager that did one or more of the above negative practices. You also know some managers who will set out to make it hard for you if you try to stand up for yourself by being honest about your involvement in a situation. Most people spend a lot of their time at work. A manager can bring out the good in you or can bring out the worst in you. What do you do if a manager is trying to define you? Always remain respectful and do the right thing, no matter what is expected. Repeat to yourself the following: *"It is in my favor and I believe in myself."* It is good to have someone to believe in you, but self-belief is the best belief. Believe in yourself.

Scenario:

Elaine was promoted to manager. She did not know what to expect, but she knew that she would be good at it. She was given a team of twenty employees to manage and train. The very first day, she started training her employees to get them started right away. She took them through the entire process and told them to practice. Their station was not yet set up, so Elaine trained them from her own computer. The next day, when they were set up at their workstations, she would encourage them. Every morning she greeted them with the following statement: "I am in it to win it today, and I won't stop until I finish it." She would ask the employees, "Are you in it to win it today?" and they would respond, "Yes, I am." Elaine was setting a positive expectation for the day. As a result, the employees worked hard and enjoyed it. Even though it was a high-stress job, Elaine employees enjoyed coming to work every day.

In the first story, the manager brought down the overall morale of the team through negativity. The manager was the cause of negative customer service reviews. The team was unhappy and did not like their results. In the scenario, Elaine built her team up through positivity. As a result, her overall team's morale was positive, and they enjoyed coming to work daily. Do not be the reason someone that you are leading fails because of your level of negativity. It is important to keep your thoughts positive so that you can give it to your team when needed the most. If you are experiencing this type of negative energy from your current leadership, keep yourself positive and you will go far in life.

Exercise:

When you are in a leadership role, try to pull out the positive in the person that you are leading. Monitor your progress and take notes of their performance.

Affirmation:

I am a positive leader, I believe in my team/employee.

Challenge:

I challenge you to practice the exercise. Try to make a difference in your team by pulling on their positive side. For a deeper experience, refer to the workbook.

CHAPTER 15

HOW PEOPLE TRIED TO DEFINE ME - PART 9

You are unique. You have different talents and abilities. You don't have to always follow in the footsteps of others. And most important, you should always remind yourself that you don't have to do what everyone else is doing and have a responsibility to develop the talents you have been given.

— Roy T. Bennett

Never allow anyone to downplay your gifts and talents or define you. Some people will try to define your every move. Yes, it is that deep. Tisha was working for a company where she was just promoted to management. She already knew that being positive and team-building would produce the best results. She was previously told by the person promoting her that she would receive a couple of veteran employees and the rest would be new employees if it could be done. Let me be the first to say that it never happened. She was given all the new employees. She was incredibly determined and was not going to focus on what she did not get. Tisha was focused more on the opportunity at hand than the broken promise. Before Tisha could do anything with her team, she had to encourage and build herself up first. You can never give your team what you don't have. Tisha built her team up and encouraged them to believe in themselves. I believe that sixty percent of your success on the job comes from believing that you can do it. It was not easy for Tisha to build up her team as they had experienced different things and were in different places in life. The more Tisha built her team's self-esteem, the better they performed. For those of you that want to know how Tisha built her team's self-esteem, I will tell you. Tisha gave each one a positive word to focus on throughout the day. The positive word that was chosen for them came from their weakness. If one lacked organization, they received the word "focused." If one lacked confidence, they received the word "confident." Every time they said things like "I cannot do this," Tisha would reiterate the word "dedicated." Tisha would remind them that they are dedicated. In the beginning, Tisha found herself doing this several times a day. Just when things were going good for them, they would go out hang with employees on other teams and come back discouraged. Tisha had to remind them not to attach themselves to that negative spirit as it was not their reality. Tisha explained that they should give the other employees positive encouragement rather than engage in the negative talk. Tisha trained her team to come in ready to work and focus on finishing several tasks before lunch. She taught about customer service each week and had different people to speak to them about customer service skills. Appreciation goes a long way. She had Employee Appreciation Day. Tisha would buy them a biscuit for breakfast, huddle up in the morning and recognize their success for the month. She told each one what she appreciated the most about them individually, and gave each one of them an award to show her appreciation. One thing it allowed her to do is build trust. When you are leading a team, they must trust you and you must trust them to have a successful outcome. Always find ways to build trust within your group, and you will see a huge difference. Tisha's team trusted her, and she trusted them. If you do not trust your manager and your manager does not trust you, it is going to be a hard-rocky road. Every employee has positivity, gifts, talents, and skills within them. It is the manager's responsibility to pull it out of them and develop it. Now that is true leadership. Tisha's co-workers were gossiping about her, lying to her, downplaying her level of success, and tried to define her. They did not like the fact that she came in new to this type of management and, within a few weeks, her team rose to the top and could not be stopped. It was so hard for them to believe that a new manager with a new team is at the top every week. The other teams could not catch her, they stopped giving the awards because Tisha's team would get it weekly. The manager's meeting went something like this: "And the award goes to Team Tisha." Out of almost thirty teams, Team Tisha won more awards than any other team. Tisha did so well, everyone in the building knew her as the team that is always winning. Then it happened, one of her supervisors talked to her about a situation about one of her employees, and Tisha was not in agreement. Tisha stood up for the employee as she did not feel that he was in the wrong. If they are wrong, she let them know that they are wrong. If they are right, she had their back to the end. Tisha's supervisor did not like it and started talking about her. He was saying things like "Tisha thinks that she is better than everyone else." He started checking her employees' work only, trying to find something wrong with it. To fulfill his own ego, he was trying to tear Tisha down. Even though her team was number one weekly, people wanted to believe a lie. Remember, numbers do not lie, people do. The experience was an eye-opener for several people as they knew the truth. Instead of just asking Tisha what her secret to success was, they rather told lies and tried to tear her down. They thought that Tisha was upset, but little did they know she was so happy. She did not allow any of these things to define who she was in life. Because the experience was so real, Tisha decided to write a manager's book to teach the above principles and instruct people never to allow anyone to define your purpose in life. Several people in the building were trying to get on Team Tisha. Other employees on other teams were seeking help from Tisha after hours. She helped them as much as she could. They complimented her daily and consistently encouraged her to keep doing what she was doing as it was working. Never allow anyone to define you, downplay your results, or make you feel less than to fulfill their own ego.

Scenario:

Thomas took a position as a manager in a huge corporation. He was excited to work and learn new things. Thomas' first day was amazing. He was particularly good at learning the job quickly. Thomas' supervisor was acting unethically by not checking the temperatures of the hot foods in the store mandated by the board of health. He would tell the assistant managers to write up employees that did not know what happened. Thomas refused to write up an employee as he was not even at work the day of the alleged incident. The supervisor got mad and told Thomas if he did not write up the employee that he would be fired. Thomas told his supervisor that he did not have to fire him as he quit. Thomas stated that he was not going to allow his supervisor to define or confine him. He stated that he felt that it was unethical to write someone up for something that was allegedly done on his off day. Thomas stated that he would rather do the right thing and quit before he allows anyone to define him or his actions. Thomas stood for what he believed in rather than someone else's beliefs.

In the first story, the supervisor tried to bring down the manager to feed his own ego. Tisha did not allow his actions to define her in any way. She felt good about who she was and focused on being a better person. In the scenario, Thomas stood up for what he thought was right at the expense of his job. It is important to make your own choices based on your ethics. Never allow anyone to make you go against what you believe in.

Exercise:

Take the right attitude today and stand up for what is true. Every day, when a situation arises, take the high road. Monitor your progress and see the results.

Affirmation:

I am a person of integrity, I am honest.

Challenge:

I challenge you to practice the exercise. Try to stand up for what is right, and it will make your life better. For a deeper experience, refer to the workbook.

CHAPTER 16

HOW PEOPLE TRIED TO DEFINE ME - PART 10

When you are content to be simply yourself and don't compare or compete, everyone will respect you.

— Lao Tzu

This time in my life was a test of my faith. All the things that I had gone through prepared me for this next experience. I was at a time in my life that I was a force to be reckoned with. I was ready and knew who I was at this time in my life. We all have those times that we are just prepared and ready to take on the world. I met a Christian lady that tried to control me every chance she got. In the beginning, my husband thought that this lady would be a good role model for me. Let me explain how it all went down. To be discreet, I will use characters to tell the story. Sharon had a daughter named Penny. Sharon often cried when telling the story of her dealings with her daughter. Penny had two children and worked 10-hour shifts overnight. Because of that, Sharon had to babysit Penny's kids. Sharon told stories often about how much keeping the kids was affecting her health and that she did not have any help with them. Every time I got on the phone with Sharon, she would always talk and cry about keeping the kids. Not knowing all sides had me sympathizing with Sharon. We had gone to visit Sharon for an extended period.

The first day was like a movie. Sharon, Penny, and I went to lunch.

The truth started unraveling. Penny was recently laid off from her job. Sharon was telling Penny about how much money was owed to her for keeping the children. Penny disagreed with the amount. Sharon got mad in the middle of eating lunch and left us. I had to call my husband to pick us up. I was shocked at her behavior and to hear that she was getting paid to babysit. It got worse. Every day, Sharon made it her business to talk about Penny negatively, as she was trying to define her. Mostly, it was only when Penny would not do what she wanted her to do. Because she could not control Penny, she would negatively talk about her, trying to confine her. I know it was about control because Penny did not do a few things that Sharon wanted to be done. She was nice and had nothing but positive things to say. It got so bad that Sharon started getting mad at me because I would not talk about Penny. I was not going to allow her negative energy to transfer to me. I remained focused. She would sit by the door and start talking about Penny asking me, "How could she do this? How could she do that?" When I would not respond and ignore her, she set out to make me pay. Her attitude was "You talk and be on my side, or I am going to do you the same way". I said to myself, "Bring it on because I can assure you that you will not define or confine me.

One day I told Penny that I would keep her kids, and Sharon was mad. She did not want Penny to go anywhere and got mad at me again for babysitting the kids. Little did I know how far Sharon would go to fulfill her need to control. First, she started lying about me, saying that she saw me smoking weed in her daughter's vehicle. Lies do not bother me, as I know who I am. I continued to focus on who I was and not what she was saying. The more it did not bother me, the angrier she got. Sharon had not walked my path and did not know what I had already gone through before our relationship. Because I would not go against her daughter, she tried to set different traps for me. She turned her family against me by lying. One of her family members called me to the side and told me that she was dealing with witchcraft against me. When she would go to church on the weekends, I guess she felt bad about the things she did in the week and wanted to apologize. I looked at that lady in the eyes and declared that she did not define me or control me. When people try to control you, do not fall into their traps out of fear. Once you allow them to control you, they will continue to control you. If you allow it, then it will become a way of life. My husband found out that this was not the relationship for me. I prayed for that lady and went my way. Who are you allowing to control you? Are you afraid to stand up because of the lies they might tell? Never allow someone to control you for any reason. If you need help to get away from a controlling person, practice in the mirror, declaring, decreeing, and building up who you are until you get the strength. Once you get the strength, stand up, move on, and do not look back.

Scenario:

Sam gave the graduation speech at graduation. Her teacher Mable helped her with the speech. Sam delivered a high powered, positive speech. She had the crowd's full attention. After the speech, they gave her a standing ovation. It was one of Sam's high moments in life. She was proud of herself. She accomplished one of her goals. She was also a talk show host for a local talk show. The things that Sam experienced at this time in her life was the most she ever did in a lifetime. Sam is always going to be at the top, as she experiences favor. Many things that she had experienced were due to favor over her life. If you are going to walk in favor, you are going to have to be ready for opposition. You are going to have to know how to ignore some stuff. You are going to have to know how to walk around some stuff. You are going to have to know how to focus on the positive things in life.

Once Sam found out that all she had to do was focus on the things she wanted versus the pain that was presented to her, she knew that she could win. It did not matter what it was, she could win, was her belief. She knew that if she focused on that mustard seed of faith that she would win every time. God said, "*All you must possess is a mustard seed of faith.*" But Sam knew if she just focused on that mustard seed of faith and nothing outside of that, she was winning. She knew that thing would come to pass. Always remember: it is not what is presented that is important. It is where you put your focus that matters the most.

In the story above, Sharon tried to control every situation and every person around her. When she could not be in control, she did evil acts. She lied, tried defining, and deceived to get her way. In the scenario, Sam focused on the positive and received more positive things that came her way. Always focus on being positive in your life so that positive will come your way as well. Never allow anyone to make you focus on the negative due to the desire to control. When you control your focus, you control your future.

Exercise:

Work on controlling your focus by focusing on the positive for a week in every area of your life. Practice and monitor your progress.

Affirmation:

I am focused on the positive things in my life, I form positive environments all around me.

Challenge:

I challenge you to practice the exercise. When you focus on the positive, you get more positive results. For a deeper experience, refer to the workbook.

CHAPTER 17

HOW PEOPLE TRIED TO DEFINE ME - PART 11

You may not control all the events that happen to you, but you can decide not to be reduced by them.

— Maya Angelou

Carissa needed to pull from deep within if she wanted to make it through this situation. She was approached about doing a management assignment for the department that she was currently working in. She decided to take the offer and help. Carissa was given 12 employees that had never done the job before, 17 that were on level one, and 1 employee that could do the job freely. This meant that Carissa would review all their work before they could move forward through the process, while the other managers had several that could just move through the process. Previously, Carissa was known for being the number one manager. Her employees were chosen this way to make it appear that she was not number one. The assignments were not lasting long, and it takes a while to train new employees, therefore skewing the numbers. Carissa had a choice: she could take the team, work harder than any other manager, as all of them had rated employees or refused the team. Rated employees could move through the process freely, as they knew the job. Carissa had to pull deep from within and muster up the strength to take on the task. She decided that it did not matter about the numbers they were trying to skew, but it mattered more about helping the employees. She knew that if she helped one employee, she did her job and could sleep well at night. Carissa knew that she was the best manager, regardless of their attempts. Carissa stopped thinking about them not being fair about the way they distributed the talent and started thinking about the lives that would be changed as a result. The one thing that could never be taken from Carissa is that she knew the truth. She saw the fruit for the first couple of days. She went into the room to find one of her employees, called him by name, and two guys raised their hand. Carissa said that both of you cannot be the same person. They both laughed as the second guy just wanted to be on Carissa's team. He sat by her team the last time that he was in the building and liked the way she trained them. Carissa had a meeting with the employees, read positive statements, and one of the previous employees stated that the positivity was missed. By the way, it was the only 1 person that had freedom to do the job with little help. One of the employees told Carissa that she was coming to see what this assignment entails. She saw that she was on Carissa's team and decided to stay for the assignment. Another employee stopped Carissa and stated that she was going to talk to the head person to request to be moved to Team Carissa. One of the employees that was currently on Carissa's team stated that she usually did not talk to people. With all the positive energy flowing on the team, she now talked often. It was refreshing to hear the positive impact that Carissa had on previous employees, soon to be employees, and employees that were currently on her team. It brought so much joy to Carissa, and she realized that this was the real reason that she was here and all the good reports were just a plus. She talked to her sister about it. Her sister challenged Carissa to look at it another way. She told Carissa that the reason these types of employees were given to her because they knew she would and could get it done. Carissa fell in love with them on the first day. She saw their potential and knew that they would do great. She started with the following on the first day and read the following to them every morning: *"I believe in you, I am here for you, you are capable of great things, you are well-respected, you are listened to, you are unique, you are worth it, I expect great things, I will never give up on you, you are worth it, I care about you, your success is my success, we are in this together, you are the reason why I am here."* - Author unknown.

It was well received. Never lose sight of the real reason that you are put in place to do any assignment. When you lose sight of your true position, you have just allowed yourself to be defined. Thankfully, Carissa knew who she was, as she had to pull deep down within to stay focused on her true purpose. Always remember if you touch and change one life, you have changed your own life. Do not allow anyone to define your level of success. Believe in who you really are and do not allow anything or anyone to change it from this day forward.

Scenario:

When driving in the car, Alexis had a wreck. She was nervous about driving in the future. Driving down the road when another car would approach closer to her, she would say that she did not want to wreck. One day, she was almost in another wreck because she kept fearing that she would get in another accident. The Bible states that the worst thing that you fear will come upon you. Instead of saying those things that you do not want, focus on the things that you do want. Start declaring and decreeing that you are safe. Say the following until you start feeling safe: *"I am safe. I am safe. I am safe."* Anything that you deal with or have an issue with, you want to say the opposite of it. Where focus grows, the energy goes. I have been told that the only thing you got to pay for is attention. Whatever you pay attention to, draws to you. This is another reason why I do not pay attention to what other people are doing. I need to be able to pay attention to my own stuff and my own things so that I can help birth my goals. Remember to focus on yourself as it is the key to making your goals a reality.

Exercise:

Practice focusing on your own goals in life. Block out all distractions and watch where you end up. Monitor your progress.

Affirmation:

I focus on my life and what it takes for me to reach my goals.

Challenge:

I challenge you to practice the exercise. Practice focusing, specifically on your own goals. For a deeper experience, refer to the workbook.

CHAPTER 18

WAYS YOU DEFINE YOURSELF
WALK IN FORGIVENESS

When you judge another, you do not define them, you define yourself.

— Wayne Dyer

Unforgiveness found itself in a sacred marriage. Gina and Paul wondered if their faith was strong enough to bring them through this situation. Gina told Paul that they must figure out a better way to deal with one another. There was certainly a disconnect between the two. I know that, at some point, everyone has dealt with unforgiveness. Gina initially said that she would forgive; however, every time a bad memory was brought up, unforgiveness would set in again and again. Paul did so many things to Gina. Gina did so many things to Paul. They could not seem to get along at one point in their life. They would get into an argument and the cycle began. Gina would yell at Paul and say things like, "You did this, you did that!" In the beginning, when Paul did things to Gina, she would not let them go. But as time went on, Gina started holding grudges and allowing unforgiveness to sink in her life. Gina started to feel that Paul was provoking her to anger on purpose. Gina took her eyes off God and put them on things that Paul was and was not doing right.

2 Corinthians 5:7 says, *"For we walk by faith, not by sight."* Looking at the negative things that Paul was doing did not benefit Gina. It

caused her to walk in unforgiveness. Gina prayed and said, "Lord, deliver me when it comes to my husband and help me to apply these principles with him." It is a beautiful thing when you can walk in forgiveness, but it takes much work. When Gina first got married, she was like, "Wow, this is so wonderful." She did not know what people were talking about. She loved her husband. She stated that she was so in love with Paul as it was the third year. It did not get rough until year 15 and 16. They almost did not make it. Gina spent every morning for a year telling her husband, "Hey, let us sow seeds in this marriage that we want to reap, let us be loving to one another, let us be nice to one another. Let us do what makes us happy." He would be like, "Yeah, you are right," but his actions did not reflect his words. When his words did not add up to his actions, Gina got mad all over again and again.

Unforgiveness started setting in and taking over. It was not until Gina was deep in it and realized it was taking over her life. Anger is another word for unforgiveness. Every time Paul said something nice to Gina, she could not receive it as she was filled with anger. Gina started to realize that she was not hurting Paul, she was hurting herself. It was turning her into an angry person that she did not want to be. She didn't even know this person anymore. She was feeling lost, as unforgiveness and anger is all negative energy. Gina was so focused on what Paul was doing wrong to her that she could not receive the things that he was doing right. Gina tried all the positivity techniques on Paul and, for some reason, just could not pull it through. It was not until Gina realized that she had given her power away by refusing to forgive. She allowed the anger to come in, which caused a spirit of unforgiveness, as it bought on a spirit of bitterness. Gina allowed herself to become bitter and, oh my goodness, it produced one argument after another argument. We all have disagreements. I get that, but they were just tolerating one another. They started pointing out each other's bad points, devalued one another and tore one another down. They realized that it was not their purpose for being together. They were defining the negative attributes in one another due to anger. They challenged one another to see the positive in each other. They began building one another up, and the angry conversations ceased. Their environment was positive, and they loved spending time together again. It is a huge difference between being negative and being positive. Many people talk about the devil, but this does not have anything to do with the devil. This has everything to do with Gina's and Paul's choices and decisions. 1 Thessalonians 5:11 says, *"Wherefore comfort yourselves together, and edify one another."*

Forgive, forgive, forgive. It is not worth it. Gina made a commitment to herself not to allow bitterness, unforgiveness, or anger to take over her life again. Gina decided not to allow the negative part of her relationship to define her any longer. She did not like the person that she had become as a result. The best thing to do would be to walk in forgiveness and just say, *"You know what I love and I forgive you, I love and I forgive you,"* over and over again until the anger leaves you. Once you realize that you do not have to pay for the things that your husband or wife does, you only have to pay for what you do, it gives you more room to focus on the positive. I know this was not a typical story that you hear about a husband and wife. This goes to show that you can bring out the negative or the positive, the choice is yours. Beware, a negative spirit can bring you down lower than you want to go and keep you longer than you are willing to stay. A positive spirit can take you higher than you could ever imagine going and keeps you surrounded with positive energy.

Scenario:

If you are a person that is easily distracted and if everything in the world bothers you, then you better start working on your level of endurance. If you are going to walk in favor, you will need to learn how to endure as favor brings out opposition, favor brings out anger in people, favor brings out jealousy, favor brings out strife and envy, favor brings out conquering and dividing. If you are not a person that can handle criticism and you cannot handle people talking about you, you better build your endurance. Endurance will help you to get over things that happen to you quicker. The higher you go, the more endurance you will need.

In the story above, Gina refused to forgive. As a result, she ended up losing herself. She was lost, as the day was long. She tried to figure out how she ended up in her current situation. Learn to forgive as it will help you to let go of the past and live for the future. In the scenario, you need to learn how to endure. If you are going to walk in God's favor, you will need to learn how to endure. If you need help building your endurance, read books and seek help from individuals that know about building endurance.

Exercise:

Read books and watch videos that will teach you how to build endurance. Always monitor your progress.

Affirmation:

I endure to the end of the process daily.

Challenge:

I challenge you to practice the exercise. When you discover techniques or ways to endure, practice to see how far you can push yourself. For a deeper experience, refer to the workbook.

CHAPTER 19

WAYS YOU DEFINE YOURSELF - BE THE BEST VERSION OF YOURSELF

As you live, your values, your sense of identity, integrity, control, and inner directedness will infuse you with both exhilaration and peace. You will define yourself from within, rather than by people's opinions or by comparisons to others.

— Stephen Covey

Always be a first-rate version of yourself and not a second-rate version of someone else.

— Judy Garland

Being the best version of yourself means that you are only in competition with yourself to do better than you did the day before. You compete with yourself. What does the best version of yourself look like? Think about it. If you use all your energy, time, and everything that you have within you to make yourself better, the best version of yourself will arise to greatness. You will become an unstoppable force.

When you are focusing on trying to be like others, you pay for it later. You will find yourself being unhappy. Being unhappy brings on several different emotions. You will find yourself indulging in shopping that you should not do, sitting in the house eating food that you should not eat, wasting away and watching TV all day, getting on the internet, scrolling through Facebook or Instagram all day. You are going to find yourself doing all these things as a coping mechanism. Now you are just coping and allowing yourself to be driven by all these different things, not seeing how they are going to add up over time. Now when these actions have added up over time, you'll look and say, "How did I get here?" I can tell you what has happened. You allowed all the things that you were doing to cope take over your life. You were becoming more like the coping mechanisms, and they were forming your life. Therefore, it is important to work on yourself and love yourself. An unhappy spirit will lead to a coping mechanism that will lead to forming unhealthy habits. The unhappy habits will create unhappy results. So, you see that trying to be like someone else is just not worth it. Once you get to really know that person, you have second thoughts about being like them.

Recognize that the best version of yourself should be your own vision, not anybody else's. Do not waste energy and time trying to live up to what somebody else wants you to be. Learn one new thing a day. Watch a thought leader on YouTube every week. Practice gratitude. Every morning or night, tell yourself 5 things that you were grateful for that day. It will make you feel much happier. Write down the things that you love about yourself. Tell yourself daily how much you love yourself. Focus on your strengths. Think happy thoughts.

A person's mind is so powerful. We can invent, create, experience, and destroy things with thoughts alone.

— DeeAnne Chomiak.

Take out time daily to work on yourself, and you will be well on your way to becoming the best version of yourself.

Scenario:

You cannot place negativity over somebody else's name or over somebody else's life, talking about them, discussing them in a negative light, and then expect positive to come over your life, that is not possible. Some are always asking the question, "Why is this happening to me?" They soon forgot about the negative things that they spoke or got in an agreement over another person's life. What you need to do is stop; if you cannot say anything positive or nice about people, try not to say anything at all. Now it is okay to recognize some things that were done to you that were not right, but always leave it on a positive note. If you can remember, speaking negative about someone else is the same as speaking negative over your own life. If you want positive, speak positive.

Exercise:

When you find yourself surrounded with people talking about other people in a negative way, learn to walk away or try to turn it into a positive conversation.

Affirmation:

I am supportive, I make a positive difference, I am connected to positive circles.

Challenge:

I challenge you to practice the exercise. When you see a person trying to be optimistic and find the positive, join in and make a difference. For a deeper experience, refer to the workbook.

CHAPTER 20

WAYS YOU DEFINE YOURSELF - KEEP THE RIGHT ATTITUDE

Gratitude turns what we have into enough and more. It turns denial into acceptance, chaos into order, confusion into clarity...it makes sense of our past, brings peace for today, and creates a vision for tomorrow.

— Melody Beattie

It is so important to have a winning attitude. A winning mindset is what you need to accomplish anything in life. Your attitude does determine your altitude. How do you have a winning attitude? A winning attitude consists of perseverance, humbleness, and a willingness to learn from mistakes. It is about viewing obstacles as challenges, not as problems. It is about knowing that there is something to learn in every situation, despite the circumstance.

How can you have a positive attitude? First, you must focus on your passions. You must focus on the thing that you want to come to pass. You cannot focus on the negative aspect of your life. You cannot focus on your negative parts and how much you need to do better. Now it is okay to acknowledge that you need to change, but it is better to focus on what you know how to do right and do more of it. Because, if you focus on the negative parts of your life and are always trying to fix those, you are going to be forever trying to fix negative areas. You must learn how to appreciate the good and bad in yourself. When you focus on the good and continue to bring good out, you will produce positive vibes. When you focus just on the negative and continue to bring negative out, you will produce negative vibes. Because the level of energy that you put out and the attitudes that you put out are looking for you. In other words, if you put out positive attitudes, then positivity is looking for you. If you put out negative attitudes, then negativity is looking for you. You cannot grow any further than you know. When negative starts to look for you, it will show up at a time that you were not expecting it and you may get it from a person that you did not want to receive it from. If that happens to you, try to put out a double dose of positivity to absorb all the negative energy. Some people do not understand that what they are looking for is looking for them. Some people put out so much negativity that they forget about how it affects other people. They often say that they did not do anything to deserve the current treatment and wonder why so many negative things are happening to them. It just means your positivity has not caught up to the negativity that you have put out. What you need to do is increase your positivity, and it will begin to change. You must think positive. You must speak positive. I will admit that some people feel that negative is easier. You can just walk out the door and get criticism. You can turn the TV on and get negative energy. Negativity is the norm, but you must make positivity your norm. You must make it your priority. You must establish the peace that you live in every day, as it is not going to fall into your lap. It is something that you have to obtain daily. How do we create that positivity? Number one, you can do it by repeating affirmations. You may not always know what to say, especially when you are just starting out. I have created an app to help you listen and recite affirmations every day, all day. It will help take positivity to the next level in your life. You can meditate on them and always listen to them. The reason why I created the app to go along with this book is so you can start getting these mindsets changed to positive and start getting the positivity within you. Once you get positive in you, it can spill out of you. Then you can start reaping the positivity. Let us keep the right attitude, produce the positive, and watch our attitude shoot for the stars. *"I am an overachiever, I am the best at what I do, I am more than enough, and will always be enough."*

It is okay to talk about situations that have happened. However, always leave it with a positive note because positivity is the key. It is the thing that is going to get you from point A to point B. I have been told that it takes 10 positive words to knock out one negative word. Now you do the math. So, you see, negativity is not worth it. If you do end up falling into negativity, hurry up and try to get out of that negativity quickly, and get into a positive state of mind. You can do that by listening to positive affirmations. Sometimes you do not know what to say. Sometimes you can get so discouraged and beat down. It is okay. Because you can put on positive affirmations by listening to my app. Listen to it over and over and over and over again, until it gets down in your spirit, to where you can start declaring and decreeing a thing. The Bible says: declare a thing, and it shall be. When you are having a bad day or feeling angry, listen to the affirmations and let it play until you are feeling better. Letting it play while you are going to sleep will help you feel better. Let it play repeatedly. Eventually, that positivity will get on the inside.

Looking at positive movies, videos that help bring out positivity, funny movies, and reading a book always makes me feel better. It works for me. Once I connect with a book, and like that book, I will read that book to completion. I will finish that book the same day, that is just me. I love books, and you do not always have to read books. You can listen to books. This book is also available in an audio version. Do whatever you need to create a winning attitude and keep a positive mindset.

Scenario:

You can have a winning attitude, or you can have a negative attitude. The choice is yours. You can make whatever choice that you want to make, but you are not free from the consequences. Never allow anyone's negative talk keep you from having a positive winning attitude. Several things can keep you from having a winning attitude, and they are as follows: negative thinking, doubt, not believing in yourself, lack of confidence, negative speaking, and talking down on yourself. Do the opposite in the above sentence to reverse the curses that you allowed through your way of living. Always be determined to have a winning attitude no matter what. With the right attitude, you can conquer the world. Attitude determines altitude.

In both the story above and scenario, it is important to keep a winning attitude. Having and keeping the right attitude is the key that unlocks the door. Positivity plays an important part in trying to keep a winning attitude. I always remind myself daily, *"I am in it to win it and I will not stop until I finish it. If I keep the right attitude, I will win every time."*

Exercise:

Get it in your mind that you are going to win and keep it until you have won. Monitor your progress.

Affirmation:

I am a winner and I keep a winning attitude.

Challenge:

I challenge you to practice the exercise. When you are losing at something this week, develop a winning attitude. For a deeper experience, refer to the workbook.

READERS CORNER

LOVING MY READERS. CONNECTING TO MY READERS. APPRECIATING MY READERS.

Acknowledging the good that you already have in your life is the foundation for all abundance.

— Eckhart Tolle

I am so grateful and thankful that you have taken the time to read this book, practice the exercises, and speak the affirmations over your life. If you have not heard this from anyone lately, just know that I believe in you. I know in my heart that God has a plan for you, and it is available to you now. Never allow anyone to take away your God-given abilities, rights, or talents. I know, everyone has a good side, and everyone has a bad side. Yes, you have made some mistakes, some questionable decisions, and even some poor choices, but it is not the end for you. From this day forward, it is especially important to start focusing on what you do right, things that you are good at, and the gifts and talents within you. You are destined for greatness. You are loved and just as good as anyone else in this world, regardless as to what anyone has to say. Have Faith in yourself and your abilities. The Bible states that you only need a mustard seed of Faith. The key is to focus on the Faith that you do have and allow everything else to fall by the wayside. I know that it is not easy, but it is well worth it. Start focusing on your strengths today. Once you make that decision, then your environment will change. The energy that you surround yourself with is important, it can and will be your power source, determine how far you go, and how long you stay. It only takes one negative statement or person to derail you. Negative energy is simply not worth it. Find positive people to talk to and if you cannot find any positive people, connect with positive authors by reading their books. Another way to connect to positivity is by listening to positive videos.

After reading this book, I have confidence that you will take your life to the next level. Self-love is the best love. Self-confidence is the best confidence. Self-help is the best help. Self-control is the best control. Self-respect is the best respect. Repeat after me and go ahead, define yourself now. *"I am loved, I am well-respected, I am confident, I am ambitious, I am positive, I am unstoppable, I am determined, I am (speak your name right here). I am the cream of the crop and rising to the top. You don't define me."* Sending plenty of love to all my readers.

For more affirmations, go to the Google Play store and Apple store to download my app that was created especially for you. The app is called *You Don't Define Me*. Use your words to build, encourage, and edify yourself and others. Join the You Don't Define Me movement and let us take control of our lives.

YOUR WORDS DON'T DEFINE ME – I DEFINE MYSELF POEM

You say that I am ugly

I say that I am Beautiful

You say that I am senseless

I say that I am Smart

You say that I am unsuccessful

I say that I am Successful

I am blessed and highly favored

Fearfully and wonderfully made

I am the redeemed of the Lord

And I say so

You say that I am unloved

I say that I am Loved

You say that I am worthless

I say that I am Accepted

You say that I am scary

I say that I am Fearless

I am made in the image of God

I am a royal priesthood

I am a chosen generation

And I am not conformed to this world but I am transformed by the renewing of my mind

That I may prove, what is good and acceptable and perfect will of God

I am the redeemed of the Lord

And I say so

You Don't Define Me!

Written by Tonya Walker

POSITIVE AFFIRMATIONS

Use your words to build up, to inspire, to encourage one another. Never use your words to hurt anyone, including yourself.

— Tonya Walker

Always Renew your Mind and Speak Positive Over your Life and Others

Positive Words and Definitions

1. I am now **abundant**
   present in great quantity

2. I am now **accomplished**
   highly skilled

3. I am now **achiever**
   a person with a record of successes

4. I am now **active**
   characterized by energetic movement

5. I am now **adept**
   having or showing knowledge and skill and aptitude

6. I am now **ambitious**
   having a strong desire for success or achievement

7.   I am now **blessed**
      enjoying the bliss of heaven

8.   I am now **bold**
      fearless and daring

9.   I am now **brilliant**
      full of light; shining intensely

10.   I am now **brisk**
      quick and energetic

11.   I am now **broad-minded**
      inclined to respect views and beliefs that differ from your
      own

12.   I am now **calm**
      not agitated; without losing self-possession

13.   I am now **capable**
      having ability

14.   I am now **caring**
      feeling and exhibiting concern and empathy for others

15.   I am now **charming**
      pleasing or delightful

16.   I am now **cheerful**
      being full of or promoting cheer

17.   I am now **clever**
      mentally quick and resourceful

18. I am now **committed**
bound or obligated, as under a pledge to a cause or action

19. I am now **dependable**
consistent in performance or behavior

20. I am now **desirable**
worth having or seeking or achieving

21. I am now **determined**
having been learned or found especially by investigation

22. I am now **devoted**
zealous in allegiance or affection

23. I am now **diligent**
quietly and steadily persevering in detail or exactness

24. I am now **eager**
having or showing keen interest or intense desire

25. I am now **efficient**
being effective without wasting time, effort, or expense

26. I am now **elated**
a feeling of joy and pride

27. I am now **elegant**
refined and tasteful in appearance, behavior, or style

28. I am now **eloquent**
expressing yourself readily, clearly, effectively

29.   I am now **energetic**
      possessing or displaying forceful exertion

30.   I am now **exceptional**
      surpassing what is common or usual or expected

31.   I am now **fabulous**
      extremely pleasing

32.   I am now **fair**
      free from favoritism, bias, or deception

33.   I am now **fair-minded**
      of a person; just and impartial; not prejudiced

34.   I am now **faithful**
      loyal and reliable

35.   I am now **fantastic**
      extravagantly fanciful in design, construction, appearance

36.   I am now **fascinating**
      capable of arousing and holding the attention

37.   I am now **favorable**
      encouraging or approving or pleasing

38.   I am now **generous**
      willing to give and share unstintingly

39.   I am now **gentle**
      soft and mild; not harsh or stern or severe

40. I am now **genuine**
not fake or counterfeit

41. I am now **gifted**
endowed with special talent or talents

42. I am now **gorgeous**
dazzlingly beautiful

43. I am now **happiness**
state of well-being characterized by contentment and joy

44. I am now **harmonious**
exhibiting equivalence or correspondence among constituents

45. I am now **healthy**
free from infirmity or disease

46. I am now **helpful**
providing assistance or serving a useful function

47. I am now **honest**
marked by truth

48. I am now **impressive**
making a strong or vivid mental image

49. I am now **incredible**
beyond belief or understanding

50. I am now **independent**
free from external control and constraint

51. I am now **innovative**
being like nothing done or experienced or created before

52. I am now **insightful**
exhibiting clear and deep perception

53. I am now **inspired**
of surpassing excellence

54. I am now **intelligent**
having the capacity for thought and reason to a high degree

55. I am now **joy**
the emotion of great happiness

56. I am now **joyous**
full of or characterized by happiness

57. I am now **keen**
intense or sharp

58. I am now **kind**
having a tender and considerate and helpful nature

59. I am now **knowledgeable**
alert and fully informed

60. I am now **leading**
a person who rules or guides or inspires others

61. I am now **learning**
the cognitive process of acquiring skill or knowledge

62. I am now **light-hearted**
carefree and happy and lighthearted

63. I am now **likable**
easy to like; agreeable

64. I am now **limitless**
a. without limits in extent or size or quantity

65. I am now **lively**
full of life and energy

66. I am now **logical**
based on known statements or events or conditions

67. I am now **lovable**
having characteristics that attract love or affection

68. I am now **loyal**
steadfast in allegiance or duty

69. I am now **magnificent**
characterized by grandeur

70. I am now **marvelous**
extraordinarily good or great

71. I am now **mature**
having reached full natural growth or development

72. I am now **merry**
full of or showing high-spirited joy

73. I am now **mighty**
having or showing great strength, force, or intensity

74. I am now **motivated**
given incentive for action

75. I am now **natural**
relating to or concerning the physical world

76. I am now **neat**
clean or organized

77. I am now **nice**
pleasant or pleasing or agreeable in nature or appearance

78. I am now **noble**
of or belonging to hereditary aristocracy

79. I am now **nonjudgmental**
refraining from making judgments, especially ones based on personal opinions or standards

80. I am now **nurturing**
provide with nourishment

81. I am now **objective**
the goal intended to be attained

82. I am now **open-minded**
ready to entertain new ideas

83. I am now **optimistic**
hopeful that the best will happen in the future

84. I am now **organized**
methodical and efficient in arrangement or function

85. I am now **original**
preceding all others in time

86. I am now **outgoing**
at ease in talking to others

87. I am now **outstanding**
of major significance or importance

88. I am now **particular**
unique or specific to a person or thing or category

89. I am now **passionate**
having or expressing strong emotions

90. I am now **patient**
enduring trying circumstances with even temper

91. I am now **peaceful**
not disturbed by strife or turmoil or war

92. I am now **persistent**
stubbornly unyielding

93. I am now **personable**
pleasant in manner and appearance

94. I am now **pleasant**
being in harmony with your taste or likings

95. I am now **positive**
   characterized by or displaying affirmation or acceptance

96. I am now **powerful**
   having great force or effect

98. I am now **qualified**
   meeting the proper standards and requirements for a task

99. I am now **quality**
   an essential and distinguishing attribute of something

100. I am now **quick**
   moving rapidly and lightly

101. I am now **quiet**
   characterized by an absence of agitation or activity

102. I am now **racy**
   marked by richness and fullness of flavor

103. I am now **radiant**
   emanating or as if emanating light

104. I am now **rational**
   consistent with or based on or using reason

105. I am now **realistic**
   aware or expressing awareness of things as they are

106. I am now **reasonable**
   showing sound judgment

107. I am now **refined**
cultivated and genteel

108. I am now **reliable**
worthy of trust

109. I am now **responsible**
worthy of or requiring trust; held accountable

110. I am now **safe**
free from danger or the risk of harm

111. I am now **satisfaction**
the state of being gratified

112. I am now **satisfied**
filled with contentment

113. I am now **secure**
free from danger or risk

114. I am now **self-disciplined**
used of non-indulgent persons

115. I am now **self-determined**
determination of one's own fate or course of action without compulsion

116. I am now **sensible**
able to feel or perceive

117. I am now **sensitive**
responsive to physical stimuli

118. I am now **sharing**
unselfishly willing to partake with others

119. I am now **sincere**
open and genuine; not deceitful

120. I am now **skillful**
having or showing knowledge and skill and aptitude

121. I am now **skilled**
having or showing or requiring special skill

122. I am now **smart**
characterized by quickness and ease in learning

123. I am now **solid**
not soft or yielding to pressure

124. I am now **sophisticated**
having worldly knowledge and refinement

125. I am now **sparkling**
shining with brilliant points of light like stars

126. I am now **spectacular**
sensational in appearance or thrilling in effect

126. I am now **splendid**
characterized by grandeur

127. I am now **spontaneous**
said or done without having been planned in advance

128. I am now **spunky**
showing courage

129. I am now **stable**
resistant to change of position or condition

130. I am now **strong**
having strength or power greater than average or expected

131. I am now **stunning**
causing bewilderment, shock, or insensibility

132. I am now **successful**
having succeeded or being marked by a favorable outcome

133. I am now **super**
a caretaker for an apartment house

134. I am now **superb**
surpassingly good

135. I am now **surprised**
taken unawares and feeling wonder or astonishment

136. I am now **tactful**
having a sense of what is considerate in dealing with others

137. I am now **talented**
endowed with talent or talents

138. I am now **tenacious**
good at remembering

139. I am now **terrific**
extraordinarily good or great

140. I am now **thankful**
feeling or showing gratitude

141. I am now **thorough**
painstakingly careful and accurate

142. I am now **thoughtful**
exhibiting or characterized by careful consideration

143. I am now **thrilling**
causing a surge of emotion or excitement

144. I am now **thriving**
very lively and profitable

145. I am now **timely**
done or happening at the appropriate moment

146. I am now **trusting**
inclined to believe or confide readily

147. I am now **trustworthy**
worthy of trust or belief

148. I am now **truthful**
expressing or given to expressing the truth

149. I am now **ultimate**
furthest or highest in degree or order; utmost or extreme

150. I am now **unbelievable**
beyond understanding

160. I am now **unconventional**
not conforming to standards

161. I am now **understanding**
the condition of someone who knows and comprehends

162. I am now **unique**
the single one of its kind

163. I am now **unselfish**
disregarding your own advantages and welfare over those of others

164. I am now **upbeat**
pleasantly optimistic and cheerful

165. I am now **valiant**
having or showing heroism or courage

166. I am now **valuable**
having worth or merit

167. I am now **versatile**
having great diversity or variety

168. I am now **victorious**
having won

169. I am now **vigorous**
characterized by forceful and energetic action or activity

170. I am now **vivacious**
vigorous and animated

171. I am now **wealthy**
having an abundant supply of money or possessions of value

172. I am now **well**
in a good or satisfactory manner or to a high standard

173. I am now **whole**
all of something including its component elements or parts

174. I am now **wise**
having intelligence and discernment

175. I am now **integrity**
moral soundness

176. I am now **witty**
demonstrating striking cleverness and humor

177. I am now **wonderful**
extraordinarily good or great

178. I am now **worthy**
an important, honorable person

179. I am now **youthful**
suggestive of youth; vigorous and fresh

180. I am now **zealous**
a feeling of strong eagerness

ACKNOWLEDGMENTS

If I would like to thank God for making me aware of the power within to accomplish my dreams. To my mother, Barbara Williams, who taught me from a child right from wrong. Even though I did not always reflect her teachings, they grew in me and one day sprouted. Never give up on your children, sow the seed anyway and one day it will sprout. I am forever grateful for my mom. To my older brother, Melvin Williams, who always expected more out of me; regardless of what he did, pushed me to do the right things. To my younger brother, Brandon Williams, for always believing me and lending a helping hand. To my baby sister, Kimberly Johnson, for always being willing to grow with me and listen to all my positive teachings. To my aunt, Carolyn Brown, who supports me in my endeavors. To Mable Pryor, my business instructor, who has always pushed me to the next level. I am truly blessed to be joined to each one of you. My love for you all grows daily.

ABOUT THE AUTHOR

Tonya Walker is a motivational speaker and author of the new self-help book *You Don't Define Me*. She is the founder of the You Don't Define Me Movement. She attended Faulkner University where she obtained a Bachelor's Degree in Business Administration. Tonya is an Administrative Manager where she continues to rise to the top with her team through the power of positivity. Her high impact You Don't Define Me principles have inspired and empowered hundreds of people to believe in themselves and pursue their dreams. Tonya was born in Daphne, AL where her father, Melvin Johnson, was the first black police officer and currently has a precinct in the City of Daphne named after him. Tonya continues his legacy of not allowing barriers or people to define her and limit what she can achieve in life.

CAN YOU HELP?

Thank You For Reading My Book!

I really appreciate all of your feedback, and I love hearing what you have to say.

I need your input to make the next version of this book and my future books better.

Please leave me an honest review on Amazon letting me know what you thought of the book.

Thanks so much!

Tonya Walker